Twayne's United States Authors Series

EDITOR OF THIS VOLUME

David J. Nordloh

Indiana University

Sarah Barnwell Elliott

TUSAS 359

Sarah Barnwell Elliott

SARAH BARNWELL ELLIOTT

By CLARA CHILDS MACKENZIE

TWAYNE PUBLISHERS
A DIVISION OF G. K. HALL & CO., BOSTON

Copyright © 1980 by G. K. Hall & Co.

Published in 1980 by Twayne Publishers,
A Division of G. K. Hall & Co.
All Rights Reserved

Printed on permanent/durable acid-free paper and bound
in the United States of America

First Printing

Frontispiece photo of Sarah Barnwell Elliott
in the garden of her house at Sewanee

Library of Congress Cataloging in Publication Data

Mackenzie, Clara Childs.
Sarah Barnwell Elliott.

(Twayne's United States authors series; TUSAS, 359)
Bibliography: p. 172–78
Includes index.
1. Elliott, Sarah Barnwell, 1848–1928
Criticism and interpretation. I. Title.
PS1589.E28Z77   813'.4   79-26452
ISBN 0-8057-7300-2

Contents

About the Author

Preface

Chronology

1. An Aristocratic Heritage   15

2. Apprenticeship   57

3. The Regional Experience   83

4. Problems of the New South   109

5. Woman's Rights   131

6. The Role of the Realist   151

    Notes and References   163

    Selected Bibliography   172

    Index   179

About the Author

Clara Childs Mackenzie was born May 28, 1931 in Asheville, North Carolina. She attended high schools in Charleston and Spartanburg, South Carolina, and was graduated from Converse College in 1951. After a year of study at the University of London as a Fulbright Scholar and another at Duke University, she received the M.A. degree in 1954. At Madison College in Harrisonburg, Virginia, she taught English courses and directed the Office of Public Relations until her marriage in 1957 to Dr. Allen H. Mackenzie.

Coming to Cleveland, Ohio, in 1958, she has taught in area high schools and colleges and been active in community affairs. Most recently she served as Assistant Director of the Center for Effective Learning at The Cleveland State University and editor of the newsletter *Learning Notes.* She has published newspaper feature articles from time to time and is co-author of *Edisto, A Sea Island Principality* (1978).

Dr. Mackenzie and her husband and four children now live in Bratenahl, Ohio, where for two years she has been doing further writing and editing manuscripts for publication. The present study of Sarah Barnwell Elliott was completed as part of the requirements for the Ph.D., which she received in 1971 from Case Western Reserve University.

Preface

It is the purpose of this study to describe and examine the small but significant body of writing produced by Sarah Barnwell Elliott (1848-1928) in light of her background and circumstances, to trace her major themes, and to see how they represent the preservation of a more liberal Southern point of view.

The search will lead back to the 1830s, when the suppression of liberalism in the South began, through the Civil War years and Reconstruction, the beginning of industrialization, the Populist movement, to the ratification of the Equal Suffrage Amendment in 1920. No attempt has been made to offer a complete historical picture; recent studies have shed much new light on the social and political problems of the South since the Civil War. Such complex and sweeping movements as Populism and the agrarian revolt are mentioned here only in association with their impact upon Elliott's life and in turn upon her writings. Since her short stories and novels were drawn largely from her own experiences and those of her family, the best of Elliott's work is social history of her region from the 1840s to 1920.

Study of a minor writer is made more difficult by the lack of serious critical commentary. In Elliott's case, there is the added problem of lack of easy access to the work itself. Virtually all of what she wrote has been out of print since 1915, when the plates of her major novels were disposed of by Holt. One collection of short stories was reprinted in 1969, but most of her stories can be found only within the brittle pages of magazines now stored in library archives. At least one story printed in the *Pilgrim*, for which no complete file has been located, may be entirely lost.

Because of her background, Miss Elliott's career was a most unusual one. Although a native Southerner of aristocratic tidewater Carolina and Georgia stock, born before the Civil War into a family of slave owners, she became a literary Realist, a diligent suffrage worker, and a supporter of liberal causes. As a regionalist she was critical of the romantic sectionalism of writers like Thomas Nelson

Page. She deliberately attempted to avoid repeating the romantic myths of the Old South and attempted to write realistically for a national audience. Her novels and stories display a wide range of settings and characters. Her stories take place on the Texas frontier, in the Tennessee mountains, the Carolina low country and piedmont, as well as in New York and Newport, Europe, and the Middle East. Her characters come from every level of society, and her rendering of several regional dialects is notable for phonetic accuracy. Her themes touch upon many of the social and intellectual issues of her day, especially the impact of Darwinian thought on religious orthodoxy, and the economic problems of the Gilded Age of American expansionism.

In many ways Miss Elliott's life is as remarkable as anything she ever wrote. Self-effacing, determined, a woman of keen mind and quick wit, she was such a new variety grafted onto native stock that more tradition-oriented women shied away from her. Her contemporaries spoke of her as "a man's woman." This sort of candid, intelligent, straightforward person, devoid of the usual "feminine wiles," became not only a role she adopted for herself, but also a character type often recreated in her work—the New Woman who was emerging in public life and the popular domestic novel as a product of the feminist movement. That this New Woman emerged in the postwar South, where women were still denied adequate education, destined only for domestic roles and sheltered from playing any significant part in public life, makes her achievements all the more unusual.

Her writing gained national recognition, and at least one book and a play were introduced abroad. Although her books commanded a wide popular readership in the leading periodicals of her day, her contributions to the development of Southern literature have been ignored or forgotten, except for one article in a collection of writings by Southern authors, mention in several unpublished dissertations, a few inches of space in *Who's Who in America*, and listings in the standard bibliographies. The present study will attempt to point out some of the reasons for this apparent neglect.

Most of Sarah Barnwell Elliott's pioneering achievements have been attributed to others. Though George Washington Cable has received credit for publishing the first postwar novel by a Southerner, with the exception of Twain, Sada Elliott's *The Felmeres* (1879) appeared a year earlier than Cable's *The Grandissimes* (1880).

Popular in its day, *The Felmeres* went through a second printing in 1886 and was issued in a new edition in 1895 by Holt.

Ellen Glasgow has often been called the first Southern woman writer to view her region as part of the national scene; yet Sada Elliott was writing for national magazines from 1886 onward and was speaking against sectionalism in literature in her book reviews and essays. Mary Johnston in *Hagar* (1913) is credited with the earliest championship of woman's rights in Southern literature, but Elliott's *The Felmeres*, "Fortune's Vassals," and *The Making of Jane* all embody feminist ideas and the character of the independent New Woman from 1879 to 1901. Elliott was also one of only three Southern writers recognized for the manner in which she wrote of the economic abuses of the agrarian revolt period. Her picture of the Southern mountaineer came as early as, but was at the same time more realistic than, the work of Mary Noailles Murfree. Her use of a Negro character as lawbreaker and her treatment of the subject of lynching in "An Incident" (1898) have been called the earliest instance of this type of Realism by a Southern writer. Her rather timid use of Naturalism in a novel of social protest, *Jerry* (1891), may have influenced bolder writers working in the same style, such as Frank Norris.

Although many of her male relatives have been recognized as writers and outstanding spokesmen in their fields, and studies as well as biographies have been written about them, no full biography of Elliott exists, and her entire career is usually summed up in the phrase "writer and suffrage leader." Yet, within this talented family, she alone may be said to have achieved a truly national reputation.

Two studies have been of great help in establishing dates and reference points for Elliott's life: Lewis Pinckney Jones's "Carolinians and Cubans: The Elliotts and Gonzales, Their Work and Their Writings," an unpublished dissertation, and more recently his *Stormy Petrel*, a study of N. G. Gonzales and the *State* newspaper, which he founded. In *Story of an American Family* (1969), Stephen B. Barnwell has collected in one place much valuable biographical information about the Elliotts.

Sada Elliott's best work lies in three of her novels and in a handful of short stories on the New South. She will be remembered as an early Realist who delineated several interesting fictional types, especially the so-called New Woman of the late nineteenth century. When detailed studies of dialect writers are made, her work will undoubtedly be included. In addition to her writings, her broad interests in the development of her native South, her example of leadership in education and woman's rights, and her work as editor and reviewer also deserve to be recognized and remembered.

CLARA CHILDS MACKENZIE

Chronology

1848	Sarah Barnwell Elliott born November 29, at Montpelier, Georgia, fifth child and second daughter of the Right Reverend and Mrs. Stephen Elliott, Jr.; named for maternal grandmother Sarah Bull Barnwell.
1852	Family moves to Savannah, Georgia. Elliott property sold for school debts.
1858	Bishops Elliott, Otey, and Polk obtain charter for a church-sponsored university at Sewanee, Tennessee.
1859	In October Sarah accompanies parents to General Convention of Episcopal Church in Richmond, Virginia. One hundred miles away, John Brown makes his raid on the U.S. Arsenal at Harper's Ferry.
1861	Federal occupation of Beaufort, South Carolina, follows capture of Port Royal, November 8, 1861. Elliott relatives become refugees.
1864	Sarah and her family leave Savannah in December on last train to depart before seizure by federal troops under Sherman.
1866	Sarah makes first long trip; visits Charlottesville, Baltimore, Philadelphia, and New York City. Contracts typhoid fever while visiting in Athens, Georgia. Asks to be called "Sada." Bishop Stephen Elliott dies suddenly on December 21.
1867	Meets Louisa Arnold; visits Arnold family at "White Hall" during the late winter of 1867-68 and again in 1868.
1867–1869	Lives with relatives at "Beechtree," Screven County, Georgia.
1869	Sada visits Louisa Arnold in July; travels to Providence and Newport, Rhode Island.
1870	Older brother John marries, accepts appointment at newly opened University of the South, Sewanee, Tennessee.
1871	In April, Sada, her mother, and sisters Esther and

	Charlotte move with John and his wife into newly built home, "Saint's Rest," at Sewanee.
1872	Sister Esther marries the Reverend Doctor Francis M. Shoup, General, C.S.A., Retired.
1874	Oldest brother, Robert, elected First Missionary Bishop of the Diocese of Western Texas at age thirty-four.
1879	*The Felmeres.*
1883	Sada's younger sister Charlotte marries Charles McDonald Puckette. Sada remains at home to care for her mother.
1884	Sada pays five-month visit to Texas, helps edit and write articles for the *Church Record.*
1886	First short story, "Jack Watson . . . ," appears in the *Current.* "A Simple Heart" appears in the *Independent* (published as book by John Ireland Company in 1887). Attends summer lectures at Johns Hopkins University in Baltimore; reported to be first female student at the University. Sada and her brother Robert depart November 27 for Europe.
1887	Visits the Holy Land. Contracts to write travel essays to pay for trip. Meets Constance Fenimore Woolson in Florence, Italy; receives encouragement to write from her own experiences. Bishop Robert Elliott dies August 26 at Sewanee upon his return from the Holy Land.
1887–1888	European stories begin to appear in the *Independent.*
1890	First story based on Southern material, "An Ex-brigadier," published in *Harper's Monthly. Jerry* serialized in *Scribner's* (published by Henry Holt and Company in 1891).
1893	*John Paget* published in wake of success of *Jerry.*
1895	Sada's mother dies June 27 at age of eighty-five. On December 31, Sada leaves Sewanee to take up full-time writing career in New York.
1895–1899	With help of her agent, Arthur Stedman, Sada successfully publishes numerous stories in *Scribner's, Harper's, McClure's,* and *Lippincott's Magazine.*
1898	*The Durket Sperret.* Attempts to go to Cuba as war correspondent.

1899	*An Incident and Other Happenings* (short-story collection).
1900	*Sam Houston* biography published.
1901	*The Making of Jane.*
1902	Returns to Sewanee upon death of sister Charlotte. Becomes legal guardian of Charlotte's sons.
1904	Play, *His Majesty's Servant,* successfully produced at the Imperial Theater, London; runs for 100 nights.
1907– 1908	Travels abroad. Winters in Rome.
1910– 1911	Serves as assistant editor of *Forensic Quarterly Review.*
1912	Unanimously elected first president of Tennessee Equal Suffrage Association. Lectures for two months throughout the East. Serves as state chairman Woman's Organization, Democratic Wilson-Marshall Committee. Writes Equal Rights Manifesto.
1913	Re-elected president of Tennessee Equal Suffrage Association. Joins national suffrage march in Washington to petition members of Congress. Addresses the Tennessee Legislature. Awarded honorary degree of Doctor of Civil Law by the University of the South at Commencement June 17.
1914	Invites National American Woman Suffrage Association to hold its annual meeting in Tennessee. National meeting November 12-14 in Nashville is turning point of suffrage movement in the state. Elliott forced to resign state presidency because of ill health.
1915	Last story published in *Scribner's.*
1918– 1928	Continues to live at Sewanee, active in university and community life. Writes reviews for *Sewanee Review.*
1928	Dies of cancer at Sewanee, Tennessee, August 30.

CHAPTER 1

An Aristocratic Heritage

To attain national stature as a fiction writer has never been an easy task. For one who happened to be born female, before the Civil War, into an aristocratic family of the tidewater South, such an attainment was highly improbable.[1]

From just such a background came Sarah Bull Barnwell Elliott, who became not only a widely read novelist and short-story writer, but also an editor, book reviewer, and playwright. In a long and fruitful life (1848-1928), she also played the role of an influential women's suffrage leader. So unprecedented was her career in the South that she was difficult to define. Biographical sketches always discussed her in relation to the men of her family, identifying her as the daughter and sister of distinguished Episcopal bishops rather than as a professional in her own right. Even her own family and close friends, with rare exceptions, found it hard to see the real Sarah behind the "bright and funloving" but sometimes acidulous spinster who, as she once wrote to a friend, had to serve as "short stop" for many people in her family as her sisters married and her brothers established their own careers.

Little has been published about Sarah Barnwell Elliott except for brief entries in biographical dictionaries and older anthologies of Southern literature, some of which contain inaccuracies. Therefore, this study begins with a biographical essay which attempts to show her life and work in relation to her family, her region, and her times.

To recognize what a truly remarkable achievement was hers, one must understand how she survived a period of national crisis and economic adversity and how she surmounted many obstacles, not the least of which was the prevailing Southern attitude toward women, especially ardent feminists. There was also the Southern indifference to literature and to its own regional writers to be reckoned with. Though public eloquence in oratory was much admired, there was almost no support for literary effort. Even so well-known a novelist as William Gilmore Simms went unrecognized in his native Charleston. The handful of men and women writers who achieved literary fame in the South before 1900 did so despite regional indifference, and found encouragement instead from editors of the national magazines of the day.

Many of Elliott's attitudes, and most certainly her writing skills, were shaped by her family background: her grandfather, her father, and an older cousin, all men of prominence in other spheres, were recognized in their day as men of letters. Ironically, Sarah Elliott was the only member of this family to earn a national—even international—reputation as a writer, but her achievements were not publicly recognized in the South until 1913, when she was awarded an honorary degree by the University of the South for her work as a writer and suffrage leader.

Among other influences which shaped Elliott was a fortunate inheritance from her parents—persons of unusual intelligence and social distinction—a legacy of intellectual ability and leadership. In addition, she seized every educational opportunity available to a woman of her situation. From her background she also derived an intense regional loyalty, a comparatively liberal point of view, and a strong and latitudinarian religious faith which preached moral betterment for all mankind.

I   *"There Are Objects More Valuable Than Wealth "*

Sarah Barnwell Elliott was born into that small, charmed circle of four thousand, the planter aristocracy of the tidewater South. Her forebears on the maternal side were some of the earliest settlers in South Carolina and Georgia, among whom was the physician Henry Woodward, first white settler of Charleston. Her ancestors numbered no fewer than four colonial governors: the William Bulls, father and son, who were successive lieutenant governors of South Carolina; Governor Robert Gibbes of South Carolina; and Governor James Habersham of Georgia. She was understandably proud of these ancestors, for they entitled her to membership in that exclusive organization known as "Descendants of Colonial Governors," as well as the Colonial Dames of South Carolina. Another ancestor was General John "Tuscarora Jack" Barnwell, pioneer Carolina Indian fighter.[2]

Her father's forebears, the Elliotts, were Quakers who came from Cornwall to settle in Charleston before 1690. A lineal descendant,

William Elliott (1761-1808), was a delegate to the South Carolina convention that ratified the United States Constitution in 1788. William Elliott had become a wealthy landowner and rice planter; he owned many acres in the Beaufort area and on Hilton Head Island, where he introduced the cultivation of Sea Island long staple cotton.[3]

By the 1840s, Elliotts, Bulls, Habershams, and Barnwells had achieved prominence as leaders in the state legislature, in the Episcopal Church (to which they all belonged), and in the local affairs of St. Helena parish, which included the town of Beaufort. Their land holdings along the borders of both South Carolina and Georgia lay in the rich bottom lands of the Savannah and Ogeechee rivers. The families were intertwined by many marriages that served to consolidate vast property holdings among them.

The first member of this family to exhibit talents as a writer and to devote himself to scholarly pursuits was Sarah's grandfather Stephen Elliott, M.D. (1771-1830), cofounder and editor of the *Southern Review*. His career was that of a latter-day Renaissance Man, for, in addition to writing and editing, he was a physician, planter, educator, and a noted botanist. Third son of William Elliott of Beaufort, Stephen Elliott was graduated from Yale in 1791 with a degree in medicine but never actually entered medical practice. Instead, he married and took up the life of a wealthy planter, studying the flora of his native region as an avocation. This study led to the publication of *The Botany of South Carolina and Georgia* (1821-1824).

Stephen Elliott's writing included essays and reviews for the distinguished but shortlived *Southern Review* (1828-1832). Writing in 1837, the British visitor Harriet Martineau commented in *Society in America* that she found the *Review* "the best specimen of periodical literature that the country has afforded."[4] While it lasted, the *Southern Review* achieved recognition for publishing papers on a wide range of contemporary issues, some of which dealt with the knotty questions of states' rights versus federal power. However, the scholarly tone of the essays, coupled with the controversial subject matter, probably limited its circulation and contributed to its demise following the Nullification Crisis of 1832.

Dr. Elliott's example of scholarly endeavor and public service undoubtedly influenced both his son Stephen, who followed him briefly as editor of the *Review*, and his grandchildren. He espoused numerous educational causes, including the founding of both the

South-Carolina College (later the University of South Carolina) and the Medical College of Charleston. In 1811 he sponsored the Free-School Bill in the state legislature to establish a statewide system of free public schools. Although it failed to receive financial support at the time, the effort earned him the title "The Father of Free Public Education" in South Carolina.[5] Moving to Charleston as head of the new State Bank, Elliott organized the Literary and Philosophical Society, served as its first president, and sponsored its first catalogue of holdings as a Library Society (1826).[6]

In an address delivered at the Medical College in 1826 while serving as a faculty member there, Elliott stated his educational aims in words which characterized the direction of the future endeavors of his family: "I seek not, I wish not to build up fortunes for individuals at the public expense; to raise up a train of idle retainers around the footstool of government; to create, as under old systems, the long catalogue of those who consume much and do nothing; but to apply the wealthy of the country to the most ennobling ideas [i.e. education]. There are objects more valuable than wealth."[7]

Dr. Elliott's words and example encouraged his nephew William Elliott III (1788-1863) to take up literary pursuits, and with considerable success, for his collected newspaper sketches, entitled *Carolina Sports by Land and Water* (1846), became a minor sports classic. It went through four editions and is still in print as part of the Abercrombie and Fitch Library (New York: Arno Press, 1967). In addition to these sketches, he wrote a group of agricultural essays privately published under the title *The Letters of Agricola* (1852) and a drama in blank verse, *Fiesco*, which was privately published in 1850.

Elliott's sketches in *Carolina Sports* are notable for their realism, depicting the gentlemanly sports and everyday life of the plantation. In at least one story, which tells about the unlawful practice of fire-hunting for deer, are found troubling hints of racial conflict and the underlying tensions of a slaveholding society. Yet Elliott never confronts forthrightly the issue of chattel slavery, for his views were those prevailing among most members of his class during the decade before the Civil War. His early use of realism, although in a tentative way, together with his vigorous narrative style and his choice of representative aspects of antebellum life, are now becoming recognized as precursors of the work of recent Southern writers like Faulkner.[8]

Depicting realistically the world of the Carolina country squire, William Elliott's work undoubtedly stood as a model for the younger generation of writers who would emerge from this talented family. When Sarah Elliott began writing in the local-color vein, her sketches and short stories utilized many of the same elements: realistic representations of plantation life, as well as characters of both races who are neither all good nor all bad. Her narrative style is spare and vigorous, and her themes, like William Elliott's, include both the lighter and darker sides of life. As we shall see, in neither writer is there seen much of the later romantic mythmaking of the postwar Southern writer, who painted picturesque but exaggerated scenes of a high-living feudal society of Southern cavaliers with baronial mansions, docile and devoted blacks, and prodigal wealth from rice, indigo, and cotton.

William Elliott's grandsons went on to become newspaper men who wrote public-spirited articles and conducted editorial crusades on behalf of economic progress in the postwar South. In 1891 N. G. Gonzales (1858-1903) founded the major newspaper in South Carolina, the *State*. He and his younger brother William served as editors of the *State* successively from 1891 to 1937, while their older brother Ambrose served as business manager of the newspaper throughout the period of progressive politics and the economic resurgence of the New South (1891-1926).[9] As contemporaries and close friends of Sarah Elliott, these cousins often corresponded with her, and she clipped and saved many of their crusading articles, suggesting a close affinity with them in a sense of public responsibility and a preference for realistic reportage.

Despite these isolated publishing successes, the older Elliotts were not regarded primarily as writers, nor did they think of themselves as such. First and foremost they were planters and professional men. The aristocratic society, which constituted the book-buying segment of the population, did not hold native literary figures in high regard, and for the most part belittled or ignored their work. A few works dealing with the comic aspects of life were widely read, such as Augustus Baldwin Longstreet's *Georgia Scenes*. But later, when Longstreet became president of the South-Carolina College, he is reputed to have expressed regrets at these literary sallies as somehow beneath him. Southern readers gave no patronage to novelists like William Gilmore Simms or John Esten Cooke, preferring instead the imported works of Sir Walter Scott. Poets of the British Isles were held in high regard, while

Southern poets like Henry Timrod maintained only a small local following and suffered severe economic privation.

Along with its neglect of native writers, the antebellum South, with its "peculiar institution" of slavery, its preoccupation with economic success and living the "good life," was neglecting all aspects of education and the arts, and with rare exceptions was culturally lagging far behind the rest of the nation. With few exceptions it was not producing outstanding thinkers, teachers, and writers. Although many local-color writers in the three decades following the Civil War would linger with fond nostalgia over these antebellum days, describing them as the high point of the Old South culture, this was in fact a time when liberal legislation and a liberal point of view were suppressed as the South, from the time of the Nullification Crisis of 1832, turned to radical conservatism.[10] In this period men of more liberal stamp, such as Hugh S. Legaré, who together with Stephen Elliott had edited the *Southern Review,* and other public figures like James L. Petigru either left the South or were forced into self-protective silence. This wave of repressive conservatism, which Virginius Dabney called the lowest ebb of the tide of liberalism in the South, cast up with it a wave of antiintellectualism as well.[11]

Sarah Elliott's father reached maturity just as this conservative reaction set in, causing him to shift from the political arena and what might have been a brilliant career in public service to the Episcopal ministry. Young Stephen Elliott, Jr. (1806-1866), had read law with James L. Petigru, one of the outstanding legal minds of South Carolina, in preparation for a legislative career. In 1832, along with other moderates and liberals, he refused to sign the test oath designed by the supporters of Nullification of the Tariff Act to purge the state legislature of liberals. Elliott retired to Beaufort to take up the private practice of law and would have remained there had not a religious revival in the town drawn him to consider the Episcopal ministry, to which he was ordained in 1836.

Elliott was shortly appointed Chaplain and Professor of Sacred Literature and Christian Evidences at his alma mater, the South-Carolina College, where he honed his considerable skills at writing and preaching and soon came to the attention of church leaders. In 1840 he was elected first bishop of Georgia, and in 1841 he moved with his family to Savannah to serve in the dual capacity of bishop and rector of St. John's Church and later Christ Church, Savannah. As bishop, he established missions for the blacks of the Georgia low country region, with their own churches and priest, on the theory that church worship and religious instruction would gradually elevate the African to responsible citizenship.

Bishop Elliott's views, considered liberal for their time and place, undoubtedly exerted a strong influence on his daughter's thinking. Sarah Elliott would later include the idea of gradual elevation of the slaves through education and religious instruction in several of her regional stories and translate it into the sphere of women in the nineteenth century, whose legal status and opportunities for education were little different from those of blacks. Her convictions of the rightness of this course of gradual evolution toward full citizenship both for blacks and for women would be enunciated in 1907 and again in an essay on "Woman and Civilization" (1910). She worked for these changes with the same fervor that her father, in his ministry, worked for educational advantages for the young women of the South along with the men, and for the moral uplift and eventual freedom of the black slave.

II *An Enlightened Upbringing*

Sarah Bull Barnwell Elliott was born November 29, 1848, in Montpelier, Georgia, fifth child and second daughter of Bishop Elliott and his second wife, Charlotte Bull Barnwell. The new baby was named for her maternal grandmother.[12]

Sarah's birthplace was the site of a seminary for young women, the Georgia Episcopal Institute, also known as Christ College, founded by Bishop Elliott in 1842 and housed at a former health resort and popular mineral spring near Macon, on land given by G. B. Lamar of Savannah. In 1845 Bishop Elliott moved his family there from Savannah to take personal charge of the school's operation, while continuing to direct the affairs of his diocese.

Establishing a school for young women was a courageous and visionary step in the 1840s, and especially so in the South, where there were few institutions of higher education even for men, and fewer still were the families concerned with the education of their female children, most of whom got what education they could at home or from private tutors. Bishop Elliott, like his father, recognized the need for liberal education of every kind in the South to effect what could not be achieved in the political arena: a more enlightened and progressive group of young men and women as future parents and leaders.

Sarah's first memories were of the scholarly atmosphere of the girls' school in its pleasant rural setting. In 1849 a contemporary, the Reverend Richard Johnson, described the school as having "extensive lawns, majestic groves, shady walks and beautiful gardens and spacious buildings. The Bishop's library," he stated, "affords an inexhaustible source of entertainment and knowledge to the pupils." Enrollment ranged from 40 to 100. The course of instruction at the college was said to be "thorough and complete, embracing every item that can contribute to fit a lady for the first stations in society." Johnson concluded that in this school "true religion, useful learning, and polished refinement are united."[13]

The school was intended to become self-supporting through agricultural enterprises carried out on land owned by Elliott, an 800-acre tract worked by slaves. Profits from farming combined with endowments and fees were to pay the salaries of an exceptionally fine faculty from the North and from Europe which the Bishop had assembled there. Elliott's biographer, Thomas M. Hanckel, reports that Elliott pledged his own lands and wealth to insure the success of the venture. However, no endowments were forthcoming, and the Diocese of Georgia was not interested in assuming the debt.[14]

When Frederika Bremer, a Swedish traveler, visited the school and met the Elliotts in 1850, she was enormously impressed by the scholarly Bishop, but also noted that he was burdened with worry. Her brief stay afforded her an opportunity to meet the bishop's family, observe the examinations at the school, and later engage in parlor games with the students. She enjoyed listening to Mrs. Elliott, "an agreeable lady, lively and intellectual," play the piano. No mention is made of the two-year-old baby Sarah, but the traveler noted her four-year-old brother, Habersham, "a good little lad," running about barefoot, and singled him out as her favorite. Of Elliott himself she could not say enough: "In him I found much of the Emersonian truth and beauty of mind, both in expression and manner, without any of his critical severity, and permeated by the spirit of Christian love as by a delicious summer air. He is one of those rare men of the South who can see, with a clear and unprejudiced glance, the institution of slavery on its dark aspect. He believes in its ultimate eradication within the United States, and considers that this will be effected by Christianity."[15] Elliott told her that he foresaw a next step when slaves would receive wages as servants, and that he "knew of several persons who were already treating their slaves as such."[16]

Elliott's concerns about being a slave owner himself were soon resolved: all his property was sold to pay the school's debts, leaving him and his family without slaves or property or even a home of their own. He moved back to Savannah in 1852 and for the next ten years served as parish priest at Christ Church to support his family while continuing his growing duties as bishop.

Although most of the family's personal papers were destroyed during the capture of Savannah in 1864,[17] a few remaining letters and reminiscences, as well as descriptions in Sarah's later stories, give a picture of her early life.

An unpublished essay written by Habersham Elliott, Sarah's brother, describes happy summers spent at Bay Point, where the children played on the beach by day and sat at night in the sand dunes, listening to a Negro storyteller's animal tales—almost identical to those later incorporated by Joel Chandler Harris in *Tales of Uncle Remus*. These traditional African tales, Habersham notes, were localized by their narrators, who selected animal characters found in the American South to replace African ones.[18] The essay describes frequent visits by the children to Beaufort, only a short distance from Savannah by train, to the home of their maternal grandmother, Mrs. John Barnwell, and to the plantations of other relatives, as well as hunting and fishing expeditions, for the boys, at least, in the St. Helena Sound or along the Savannah and Ogeechee rivers.

The opening paragraphs of an Elliott short story, "Beside Still Waters" (1900), give an even more detailed view of domestic life in this coastal town of cotton and rice barons:

This town of Kingshaven [Beaufort] was the private property, almost, of a few large clans of planters, more or less nearly related. They kept their horses and dogs, their rowboats and sailboats; they owned hunting islands, and islands that were little more than sand-bars, where in summer they marooned for the sake of the sea-bathing, spending the winter months on their plantations. Their wine, their silver, their furniture and books and gout and church were standard, and from the mother country, sent over in exchange for the silky, long-staple "sea-island cotton." All these customs and habits and manners were of ancient date,—had been held sacred by everyone of the many generations that lay asleep about the walls of the old church built of English brick,—and having been handed down intact, Kingshaven could not change.

But if the days followed each other in peaceful monotony, happy in having no history; they were not idle days. There were the seasons, with their planting and reaping. There were the innumerable aunts and uncles and grandparents and cousins out to the fourth and fifth degrees, dining and teaing and visiting from house to house, and keeping kindly and conscientiously abreast of each other's affairs. There were friends coming and going from the outside world, and all manner of simple and plentiful hospitality to be used toward them. There were books and flower-gardens and beautiful kinds of embroidery and important kinds of sweetmeats; for there were noted housekeepers, after the prodigal Southern fashion, in this town, whose recipes for certain things were of a wide and enduring reputation, such as the making of exquisitely carved orange preserves and the various ways of preparing crab and terrapin. Then there were missions, foreign and domestic, and politics, growing darker and more lurid as the years drew toward the furnace of the War of Secession.[19]

Even so crusty a critic as H. L. Mencken, who in later years would decry the absence of Southern literature and the arts in "The Sahara of the Bozart," conceded that in the South of earlier years "some attention was given to the art of living—that life got beyond and above the state of a mere infliction and became an exhilarating experience." The Southerner "liked to toy with ideas. He was hospitable and tolerant. He had the vague thing that we call culture."[20]

Within family letters as well as Habersham's retrospective essay is the constant awareness of slavery and the position of the black person in the society: among these Carolina planters the slave was a familiar presence, often respected, even beloved and trusted, but always separate and never equal. Unlike many of their neighbors, the Elliotts expressed privately in conversation and correspondence grave concerns about the institution which they had inherited. As early as 1804 Dr. Stephen Elliott had expressed in a letter his wish to be rid of his rice plantations because of the malaria and yellow fever that took their toll on his slaves as well as his family.[21]

According to Habersham Elliott, the Elliott uncles, aunts, and cousins had for many years transgressed the strict slave laws which forbade the teaching of reading or keeping of accounts by slaves. Habersham's grandfather had had a slave overseer named Anthony who kept all plantation accounts, and other family members paid an annual fine for keeping a black "driver" on their plantations instead of a lower-class white overseer. The Elliotts had organized schools for house servants, and one unmarried aunt dedicated herself to the schooling of all the people on her remote Ogeechee River plantation.

Though privately troubled by slavery, Bishop Elliott preached gradualism and eventual emancipation "when they were ready for it," defending slavery while it lasted as an institution ideally suited for Christianizing the African. When he was made bishop he called for "a body of well instructed colored communicants in every Episcopal Church," and extended missionary work among the Indians as well.[22] His Ogeechee Mission, which provided slaves their own church and priest for the all-black congregation, was viewed as an outstanding example of missionary work in its day.[23] When emancipation came in 1863 the bishop asked the parishes under his jurisdiction to help the freedman, strongly expressing his approval of abolition: "As for me and my race . . . I rather rejoice in it."[24]

Sarah would acquire through her early and close association with these black people affection and understanding of them as individuals, but she found difficulty in dealing with the enormous problems of a disadvantaged race. In several stories, blacks as main characters are for the most part treated sympathetically; each is portrayed as an individual with distinctive traits, not merely as a picturesque stereotype. One of the best portrayals shows the sensitivity and devotion of the black woman Kizzy to her former mistress while living as a refugee far from home in the short story "Faith and Faithfulness" (1896).

Two factors predominate in writings of the Elliott children about these early years: the impact of religion upon their lives and the need to gain a living by their own intellectual effort rather than by the agricultural labor of others. Weekly church attendance, religious instruction through their father's sermons, and daily Bible reading at family prayers were part of their upbringing. Their father's weekly preparation of sermons was an example of regular intellectual discipline for them all. The power of the spoken word was ever before them as well, for Bishop Elliott was renowned for his eloquent and often fiery sermons.

"Living by one's wits" had become a necessity for Bishop Elliott's family long before the Civil War, when other members of the family lost their property and were forced to cast about for ways of making a living. Skill in oral and written expression had been inherited and was consciously cultivated in this family, as were music, the love of poetry, and the study of literature, history, and the natural sciences. The Elliotts possessed the highest ideals of eighteenth-century enlightenment, coupled with a strong sense of social responsibility. They were proud, highly cultivated but not ostentatious, and they

valued intellectual and spiritual attainments more highly than personal fortunes. As Sarah's grandfather had once acknowledged:
"There are objects more valuable than wealth."[25]

While the political stormclouds gathered elsewhere in the nation,
daily life for the Elliott children was both cheerful and secure
despite their genteel poverty. Into the already large family of five
children another daughter, Charlotte, had been born in 1850. Their
modest income was supplemented by gifts of foodstuffs and game
from relatives living on nearby plantations. In Sarah's family frugal-
ity became a lifelong habit. Though possessions were few, the
children never wanted for books, music, and social entertainments,
which they enjoyed on extended visits within the large family
network centering around Beaufort.

Higher education for the older sons in this family of potential but
limited means was an enormous problem. With the help of funds
from an uncle, the oldest son, Robert (b. 1840), began his studies at
the South-Carolina College in 1858. Affectionate letters flowed back
and forth between family members. Writing to her son away at
college, Charlotte Elliott frequently mentioned "the little girls" and
their school activities, presumably studying at a neighborhood
"dame school." She wrote of how impatient the youngest sister was
to move ahead with Sarah, then ten years of age, and she added,
"Sada frequently says, 'I declare I miss Rob so.' "[26]

There were no funds to send the girls to school, but each of
Sarah's brothers was prepared for one of the professions. Robert,
like his father, studied for the ministry, while John (b. 1841), the
second son, studied medicine. The college careers of both boys
were interrupted by the Civil War, in which each served. Habersham (b. 1846), the youngest son, was most affected by the war,
through interruption of his studies. Only fourteen at the outbreak of
hostilities, he also managed to enlist before the end of the war.
Robert became a lieutenant in the Savannah Volunteer Guard and
served as aide-de-camp to General Alexander Lawton. John was
commissioned a lieutenant in 1863 and assigned to Maxwell's Light
Battery in Savannah. At one point toward the end of the war, John is
said to have discovered his younger brother Habersham, by then a
seventeen-year-old recruit, lying ill and unconscious of fever along a
Georgia roadside.[27] The incident and what followed became part of
the family legend, remembered by Sarah and written into a short
story, "Jim's Victory," published by *Book News* thirty-five years
later.

Following news of Lincoln's election in November 1860, the Ordinance of Secession was signed in Charleston on December 20. Less than a month later, federal gunboats were steaming into Port Royal Sound below Beaufort. That same month, Habersham, about to go with his father to Beaufort to determine the fate of relatives there, described to his older brother seeing "two men-of-war off Tybee." In the same letter he wrote of another vessel at the mouth of the Ogeechee River, and of troops from Savannah being ordered to Virginia as the South mobilized for war.[28]

On November 7, 1861, began what the Negroes later referred to as the "day of the gun-shoot at Bay Point." The Beaufort area had been singled out for capture because it had become a center of secession activity under Robert Barnwell Rhett. Around the middle of November the planters began moving their families and possessions out of the area of likely federal occupation, taking a few loyal house servants and leaving the rest of their vast property to be pillaged by the remaining slaves. Federal troops moved in to restore order and to salvage part of the cotton crop. A plan was devised whereby land was redistributed into small farms and given to the former slaves for cultivation. This plan, which came to be known as the Port Royal Experiment, served as a laboratory for dealing with freedmen during Reconstruction.[29]

The Barnwell and Elliott homes were among those deserted by their owners, who fled to avoid capture. They remained throughout the war in Flat Rock, North Carolina, or other remote areas where they had summer homes or relatives. Bishop Elliott and his family stayed in Savannah throughout the war, where the bishop continued to preach and carry on his ministry, according to acquaintances who visited there. A family wedding was held in Savannah on January 7, 1864, when their eldest son, Robert, was married to his cousin Caroline Elliott, daughter of Ralph Emms Elliott of Savannah. The family left on the last train out of the city in 1864, before Sherman's arrival.[30]

Some semblance of family life must have been maintained throughout these turbulent years. Sarah was kept at home to learn the three R's, along with her sisters Esther (b. 1843) and Charlotte, called Dawtie. Her time was occupied with music lessons supplied by her musically talented mother, with constant reading, and, at about the age of twelve, with her first attempts at writing.

Except for a group of letters describing wartime experiences written by the Elliott sons, nothing illuminates conditions in Savannah during and after its occupation in December 1864, nor the privations of Sarah and her family as war refugees. Others have described the extensive damage done to the city and the problems throughout lower Georgia in the months following Sherman's occupation. Travel was almost impossible. Food was hard to obtain in the winter of 1864-65, since food supplies had been confiscated and farm animals slaughtered. Heavy rains and lack of labor prevented the planting of crops. A severe typhoid epidemic also broke out in the spring. Families were separated, surviving as best they could with friends or relatives. Social and political life was at a standstill, and even the courts could not convene to administer justice until 1866.[31]

Sarah was to see little of her father during the war years. Throughout 1860-1865 Bishop Elliott was traveling constantly, trying to deal with church problems. Soon after secession, the Southern dioceses had voted for separation from the national Episcopal Church, and Elliott, as the senior bishop of the Southern Council, had been elected Presiding Bishop. Staunchly partisan to the Southern cause, he preached patriotic sermons and prayed for a Southern victory. After the fall of the Confederacy he even offered to share internment with Jefferson Davis in the federal prison at Fortress Monroe. Despite his sectional loyalty, he nonetheless saw the wisdom of reconciliation between the two halves of the divided Church; Elliott led the Southern dioceses to effect without rancor a merger with the national Church. Other denominations similarly divided by the war still remain split into sectional jurisdictions today.

Not only did he work tirelessly for the Church, but, until the time of his death, Bishop Elliott continued his efforts to improve education in the South. Most notable had been a joint effort with Bishop (General) Leonidas Polk of Louisiana and Bishop James Harvey Otey of Tennessee to found and endow a church-supported university in the South. By 1858 a charter had been secured, and Elliott had helped raise more than half a million dollars in endowments. In 1860 a cornerstone had been laid on Sewanee Mountain in Tennessee, where the future university was to rise, but at the end of the war, two of the founding bishops were dead, the pledged funds had evaporated, and even the cornerstone had been blown up in battles fought over the area. In 1866, as sole surviving founder, Bishop Elliott called together the trustees once more. Deeds to the land were located and plans were scaled down to include a preparatory school, a College of Arts and Sciences, a small graduate school, and a school of theology. Construction was begun, and classes opened in 1867.[32] Elliotts have continued to hold close ties with the university down to the present.

Bishop Elliott did not live to enjoy his great accomplishment. The heavy responsibilities imposed by relief efforts and the postwar problems of his church, as well as the works in behalf of the University of the South, took their toll. He died suddenly on December 21, 1866, in Savannah and was buried on Christmas Day with many honors at Laurel Grove Cemetery near the Savannah River. A glowing eulogy on his life and work was delivered by Bishop Richard H. Wilmer of Alabama.[33]

The death of her father dealt Sarah Elliott the most severe of a series of blows in what had otherwise been a secure, loving, and on the whole enlightened upbringing. The effects of growing up in genteel poverty, then the war and living as a refugee far from home, followed by the sudden death of a parent whom she idolized could well have devastated a gentler nature. But Sarah, molded by family traditions, education, and religious convictions, seems to have sustained the shock with a maturity beyond her years, and strengthened her resolve to make something of her life despite adversity.

III *"I Might Be Persuaded to Publish . . ."*

The dreary months of mourning which followed the death of a beloved and revered parent were lightened somewhat by the return to near-normalcy as the family once again began to move about in the subdued social life of Savannah. Mrs. Elliott and the girls found a temporary home with relatives at Ralph Elliott's plantation, still intact along the Ogeechee River in Screven County. Sarah was allowed to journey into town, to visit with friends on neighboring estates, and to attend several social functions during the holidays of 1867.

In the autumn of her eighteenth year, shortly before her father's death, Sarah had traveled with relatives to Charlottesville, Baltimore, Philadelphia, and New York, where among other new experiences she attended her first opera performance. She wrote an enthusiastic description of her adventures to her brother: "Riding, driving, boating, and walking, and good fare," she wrote, had all benefited her health and afforded a needed change. "Talking of change, I think this one has done me more good than any since I left

home as I now weigh 101 pounds and all my bones are cov-
ered. . . ."[34] She ended the letter with a request to be called
hereafter not Sarah but Miss *Sada* Elliott. The butterfly had
emerged with a new look and a new name to match. *Sada* she would
be called the rest of her life.

The following autumn Sada went to visit with the Huger family in
Athens, Georgia, where she was suddenly stricken with typhoid
fever and lay dangerously ill for weeks. Her mother and her
physician-brother John hurried to Athens to look after her, plying
her with "a regular course of whiskey toddy and beef tea day and
night" until she was sufficiently out of danger to be moved.[35] The
long fever wasted Sada's already slight frame and caused her to lose
most of her hair—a source of much embarrassment at an awkward
time for an adolescent.

Though 1867 had been a year of mourning, 1868 was made
brighter by Sada's acquisition of a close friend. It was her first
girlhood friendship of any duration, and one which opened many
doors for her socially. More important, it gave her a whole new set
of experiences and views of life. The friendship inspired an outpouring of letters and diary entries which afford the first extensive
view of Sada's emerging personality.[36]

The newfound friend was Louisa Caroline Arnold, daughter of
Samuel Greene and Louisa Caroline Gindrat Arnold. Arnold, an
attorney, had served as lieutenant governor of Rhode Island and as
U.S. Senator from that state. The Samuel Arnolds made their home
in Providence but came often to Georgia during the winter months
to visit Mrs. Arnold's family and to look after their property. Mrs.
Arnold's mother had inherited property in Georgia, and was naturally strongly partisan to the Southern cause.

It was during a Christmas visit by Louisa to her grandparents in
1867-1868 that the friendship with Sada developed. The two girls
shared holiday parties and Sada paid a visit to "White Hall," one of
the Arnolds' Georgia plantations, throughout most of January 1868.
An exchange of letters continued through the summer and fall after
Sada had returned to Screven County. Sada visited at "White Hall"
once more after Louisa returned to Rhode Island, and in the
summer of 1869 Sada was invited to Providence. Her trip to
Providence and on to Newport during the height of the season at the
famous summer resort provided exciting new experiences, none of
which was forgotten. No experience was ever lost to Sada. All she
observed, even the names of some of those whom she met, returned

to mind as she wrote her first novel, *The Felmeres* (1879). Other scenes, names, and incidents were used in *The Making of Jane* (1901).

One may surmise that this friendship of a wealthy and rather conventional young woman with an emotional and imaginative young Southerner turned out to be somewhat one-sided. Louisa wrote in her diary all the details of Sada's visits, their parlor games and pastimes, and preserved all of Sada's letters. These provide the only written traces from this period of a sensitive young woman struggling to make friends and to establish her own complex personality in a period of imposed isolation and poverty.

Visiting with Sada in 1868 at "Beechtree," a plantation where the Elliott women were then living, Louisa recorded being somewhat overwhelmed by the intellectual tone of the family conversations, especially on the subject of poetry, of which they were all fond. "'I wish I knew as much as they," she remarked wistfully. Louisa was favored with a reading of Sada's first "novel," a rambling fictional biography entitled "Rest Remaineth." Later the remnants of the never-published schoolgirl novel were used for a scrapbook over which poems, clippings, and book reviews were pasted by the author, who had the critical good sense to recognize this first bit of juvenilia for what it was. Out of that first effort, all that ever came to print was the title "Rest Remaineth," given to a short story published in the *Pilgrim* in 1900.

On Sada's side, some of the notes dispatched from "Beechtree" or "The Lodge" to "White Hall" reveal a good deal about the writer. Whether because of her serious illness, her unusual intelligence, her year of mourning, or her sheltered life overly occupied with books, Sada seemed to hold herself in low regard and thought herself quite different from her girl friends. Unintentionally, perhaps, she was beginning to reject for herself the role of a conventional Southern woman. She wrote to Louisa in March 1868: "I don't blame people for not liking me. I am only surprised if any do, and if I am liked it is generally because I have the power [of self expression] and am bitter and sarcastic and therefore amuse them for the moment. I know that I can count two perhaps three friends besides yourself and only those are so because they don't know me thoroughly, which is I fear your case. I have some among the men I know, and am thankful for it. They make better friends than women do, in the long run. . . ."[37] The stream of letters that followed Louisa home to Providence in June of that year make a perfect litany of loneliness. Sada's older sister Esther (Hesse) was spending the summer in upcountry Georgia with friends; the brothers were all away from home struggling to establish themselves in their various professions; Charlotte (Dawtie) was attending school. Sada was left alone to wander about the house, moping and "remembering happier things," especially those young men who had paid her their attentions at the Christmas parties in Savannah the year before. In one note she added, "I am worse lonely than ever my dear for they have stopped me from going for the mail saying it is not safe for me to ride about by myself."[38]

By this time the South was in the throes of Radical Reconstruction. The attorney for Louisa's future in-laws, the Appletons, wrote of "armed bands of negroes—roaming the plantations and having stolen all the rice."[39] Inflation ran riot, there was little or no mail service, and a state of near-anarchy existed. The presence of U.S. military forces was of some help in restoring and maintaining order in Georgia, but there remained much bitter feeling, lawlessness, and anonymous killing of Negroes by lynch mobs. Southern women were caught between fear of the wandering freedmen and hate for their so-called protectors.[40] The attorney explained that part of the problem stemmed from the fact that former employers, having no cash, could not pay the freedmen's wages; the workers therefore helped themselves to rice and other goods in lieu of payment.

Although virtually imprisoned at home by the increased racial violence, Sarah did not entirely neglect her education. Books from the family library were available to her. In addition to music and drawing, she was learning some French. Her reading at this time included the currently popular English novelists, American authors including Hawthorne and Emerson, some history, philosophy, and theology, and a great deal of poetry. She wrote to Louisa in July 1868: From the 12th of May to the 12th of July, a space of two months, I have read 4,350 pages of History and 2,300 pages of miscellaneous books—the total amount being 6,650 pages. . . . I have kept a most strict account of all that I have read. Tis true I have not done much else except practicing [on the piano] two hours a day. . . . My writing progresses slowly, although I have finished only a year and begun another called 'My Life.' Taint mine though only an imaginary one. You shall have the pleasure of plodding through them all though when I see you. I wish you joy of the job. . . .[41]

A much brighter letter to Louisa followed this one a month later.

The stay in the country had been broken by a trip to Rome, Georgia, for the ordination of Sada's oldest brother Robert to the Episcopal ministry:

Congratulate me on having finished my sojourn in the wilderness. At least for a while. Mama at last determined to bring me up to Rob's ordination. You may imagine how glad I was. Why have you not written me . . . have you gotten tired of my prosy letters? or have you become so immersed in the Newport gaities as to forget me? . . . I am having a very nice time here—not quite so charming as last winter in Savannah but still it is a Paradise to Screven—poor old Screven—how glad I was to leave it. My stay there has made me much graver—even I can see it and feel it. Minna persuaded me to let her take home one of my novels to read—so I gave her "Rest Remaineth," do you remember the day in the Billiard room? how very foolish we were over the imaginary woes of the most unfortunate hero and heroine—how silly we were. I might be persuaded to publish one of these days if I improve any, but I think it would be the most rediculous [*sic*] nonsense to publish now—all I could do would be to disgrace my name and I don't care to do that—but if ever I do such a foolish thing as publish—you shall be among the first to receive a copy. . . .[42]

One of the bonds which cemented the friendship had been a brief courtship between Louisa Arnold and John Mackay Elliott, Sada's cousin. This bond was severed in 1870 when Louisa became engaged and soon married George Lyman Appleton of Savannah. Another more serious breech resulted from Sada's self-acknowledged habit of forthright and often bitterly sarcastic expression of her views. While in Providence the summer of 1869, she apparently had expressed herself rather too forcefully on the South's position during the war. The remarks brought on a squabble in the Arnold household because of the family's divided loyalties, the grandmother being loyal to the South and Louisa's mother to the Union. When news of the incident reached Senator Arnold in London, he wrote home a most stern letter explaining the personal embarrassment which would result to him if pro-Southern sentiments in the family of a United States senator became known. Arnold's unkindest remarks were reserved for "Saida," his daughter's outspoken young friend. He urged his daughter in the future to denounce the madness of slavery and Southern "rebellion" in no uncertain terms if the subject were ever introduced while his daughter was in the South. The attempt to destroy the Union, he said, "was the greatest crime in history, and no feeling of courtesy should permit of its extenuation for one moment . . . ."[43] Unwittingly having prompted an outpouring of anti-Southern sentiment in the senior Arnold, Sada must then have fallen out of favor with the family. The correspondence ceased soon after, and the friendship lapsed, casting Sada into deep depression over her lost friendship. The two friends probably never saw one another again.

IV   *"I Never Was Made for a Saint"*

For nearly four years following the death of Bishop Elliott in 1866, Sada and her mother and sisters had lived with first one relative and then another since, with her father's death, the family had lost the use of the rectory, the only home they had. But now their fortunes improved. In January 1870 Sada's brother John, his medical training completed, moved his bride, Lucy, along with his mother and sisters, to Sewanee, Tennessee, where he had accepted an appointment at the newly opened University of the South. At first they were accommodated in one of the college dormitories. In a few months, with capital drawn from his mother's meager trust fund, John designed and built a new house for them all, which they called "Saint's Rest." Next door was a small dwelling—quickly dubbed "Sinner's Hope"—that housed a dozen university students, who would board with them.

Years later, in a rather rambling unpublished novel entitled "Madeline," Sada wrote of a proud Southern matron, much like her aristocratic mother, who felt deeply humiliated by the necessity of keeping a boarding house to make a living. Yet taking boarders was one of the few respectable ways for a nineteenth-century woman to augment her family income. Since other families at Sewanee did it, Mrs. Elliott managed to swallow her pride and adjust to the times.

Running a boarding house did not prevent Mrs. Elliott from maintaining the spirit of Southern hospitality at her Sewanee home, however, and she kept "open house" every Sunday afternoon in the style of her tidewater ancestors, a practice continued by Sada long after her mother's death. Her children recalled in later years how Mrs. Elliott presided over these gatherings, seated in the carved oak chair which had belonged to her husband, a regal matriarch in her starched white widow's cap and bearing a marked resemblance to Queen Victoria, whom she admired.

Having a home once more, albeit a busy, crowded one, brought to Sada, as to the other family members, a sense of security, and with it, her mood brightened. The dark tone of some of her letters for the past two years was gone. There was no more talk of death, of premature old age, of hopes denied. In a long and wittily impertinent letter written to her brother Hab in April 1871 she savored the delights of unpacking "the blessed old books. . . . I handled them just as if I was shaking hands with some old friends, whom I have not seen for some time. We will be all ready when you come," she continued, "and you will find it home, home as you remember it, the same old kernel, only in a pretty new shell."[44]

In the same letter Sada took mock inventory of herself, giving the only real self-portrait we have of her, characterizing herself as destined to be something less than a saint:

Do you know, can it be true that you have not heard that I am going to desert society and make tracks for the sisterhood? Leave "the world and worldly things beloved" and retire to a church home for old maids. Do you not realize that I, having reached the age of 22, have "quit struggling" and quite sneer matrimony down. . . . When a woman gives up all idea of matrimony, she either turns saint or woman's rights, and as the name of Elliott has never yet been disgraced, I do not propose to find my vocation in the Forum. The only thing left me then is Saint, "picture it, think of it, Saint Sarah." It goes against the grain very much. I never was made for a Saint.

She went on to describe all their neighbors, often comparing different ones to characters from Dickens. Of the Elliott household she said playfully:

Next to Mr. Judd's comes the Elliotts, a very queer sort of family to tell the truth. They have just moved into their new house, which is a decent affair on the whole. The style is Gothic, color pale lemon, trimming white, the lot is quite a nice one though not fixed up yet. On the South side of the big yellow house is a little yellow house occupied by ten youths. The place is named "Saint's Rest." The family are six in number, not counting the baby. The first is Mrs. Elliott—a most charming old lady of the old school, perfectly indescribable, intensely pleased with and proud of all her children except the second daughter Miss Sada of whom she is a little doubtful. . . . Sixth comes Miss Sada, not at all lacking in the family trait of self-complacency, very contrary to everyone and everything, and very obstinate, rather selfish and supercilious, quite a tease, not very intimate with anything but her own shadow . . .

After the marriage of her sister Esther to the Reverend Francis Asbury Shoup in 1872, Sada was obliged to assume greater domestic responsibility. Nevertheless she found time to send out a stream of letters and to work at intervals on her fiction-writing. Not a single line of her work had yet found its way into print. But between "saint or woman's rights," she was beginning to evolve for herself a third way of life, that of observer and recorder of experience. The 1870s constituted her real apprenticeship.

Two major events within one year's time brought satisfaction to all family members: the election of the eldest, Robert Woodward Barnwell Elliott, as First Missionary Bishop of Western Texas in 1874 and the marriage of the youngest son, Habersham, in 1875. Gradually the excitement of moving into the new house, of family weddings, and of her brother Robert's consecration began to subside. Sada wrote of "that everlasting baby, howling in the next room" making concentration difficult. Yet somewhere in the midst of domestic turmoil and the small daily frustrations of living in a large family, she found a place and a time to write. A few hours each day were devoted to her work, work that alone gave shape and meaning to her private life. Bit by bit she was developing a terse, professional, public style in her writing—a style that would sell.

Finally, in 1878, Sada decided that it was time to attempt publication of some of her manuscripts. Her first novel, *The Felmeres*, was accepted by D. Appleton Company of Chicago and readied for publication in the spring of 1879. It was in all the bookstores by June, a 357-page edition which sold for $1.50. Her writing career was launched at last, in the author's thirty-first year.

Family and friends were profuse and generous in their comments, although no one seemed to express any surprise that Sada *had* published successfully; it seems to have been more or less expected of her. The wisest of these letters was from Habersham, who as always seemed to understand Sada best and to say what she most needed to hear. He acknowledged that her gift for writing would allow her "to preach to whole populations" as no one in the family had yet done. Hab further cautioned her to conserve her strength, for it was her duty to preserve her health; her chosen profession would be a demanding one.[45]

Sada kept in her notebook every review and congratulatory letter sent to her and from them drew sufficient encouragement to go on writing. She continued, meanwhile, to divide her time as always among her work, her family, and the life of the university community, directing the boarding house and looking after her mother and younger sister. Having given up the idea of matrimony, she seemed still to vacillate between her own polarities of "sainthood or woman's rights." These appear as themes in her first novel and as the chief attributes of her heroine Helen Felmere. In a work full of religious speculation, the poor martyr-heroine appears less a flesh-and-blood woman than a vehicle for discussing the legal and moral concerns of women in the nineteenth century: marriage, property, and the control of one's own destiny. Helen Felmere marries less for love than for duty, is denied the right to rear her own child as she chooses because of her religious beliefs, and has as her only weapon her property, which her relatives try to take from her. Although cloaked in religious arguments, a great many woman's rights issues are brought out in the complex marital problems of the heroine.

V   *"In the Literary World I Am Just Cutting My Teeth"*

The next decade would bring Sada Elliott opportunities for travel, study, and personal growth, which in turn would contribute new themes and a greater variety of characters and settings to her writings.

On December 27, 1883, her younger sister Charlotte was married to Charles McDonald Puckette, a professor of ancient languages at the University of the South. The happy occasion presented a rare opportunity for the whole family to be reunited. Bishop Elliott came from Texas to perform the ceremony; John came up from New Orleans, where he was teaching during the winter term; and Habersham, now a civil engineer, arrived from his railway construction project, which was putting down the Memphis and Vicksburg Railroad line. Meanwhile, Esther and her husband had recently returned to Sewanee, where for the next nine years Dr. Shoup would teach courses in mathematics, physics, and engineering at the university.

Sada was invited to accompany Robert back to Texas for a long visit after the wedding, which had no doubt reminded her acutely of the fact that she was now the only unmarried member of her family. Early in the new year, they set out for San Antonio, where Sada was soon traveling about with the bishop on his pastoral visits to many parts of his far-flung diocese. While she was there, her brother suggested she might try putting her writing talents to practical use reporting his activities for the diocesan newsletter, the *Church Record,* to which he as bishop was principal contributor.

Gradually during her four-month sojourn Sada took over many of the reportorial duties of the newsletter. On one occasion she wrote a detailed account of a trip through northern Mexico, where she found the colorful central plaza and soft-spoken people of the town of Monterrey especially appealing. The travelers moved on to Saltillo and then home by way of Laredo. Sada's description of the journey swelled the February 1884 issue of the *Church Record* to an unaccustomed twelve pages. In the March issue a mildly satiric two-and-half-column article entitled "To Whom It May Concern," signed with the initials "S.B.E.," discussed proper behavior in church—decorum being somewhat lacking in the frontier churches. Other articles signed simply "Visitor," written in the unmistakably vivacious style of "S.B.E.," described the towns of Corpus Christi and Gonzales, offered notes on the annual convention of the Episcopal Church at San Antonio, and told of a visit to St. Mary's girls' school (which was run by the church), along with other travels and activities of the bishop.[46]

After the June issue, the church paper returned to its former dull subject matter, long lists of clerical appointments and official acts. Sada, the "Visitor," had gone home. For a brief interval her presence had enlivened the pages of the little paper. More importantly, the visit had restored her gaiety of spirit and had given her new confidence in her ability. Her brother wrote in a letter to his mother of Sada's having livened up even the accounts of funerals: "If you hear the noise on the mountain you will have to come over and manage your gay bird," he concluded.[47]

Back in Sewanee the "gay bird" began shaping her experiences into stories which would attempt to capture in fiction the flavor of the frontier country she had visited. Immediately encouraged by acceptance of one of her pieces, "Jack Watson—A Character Study," in a national magazine, the *Current,* for September 1886, she began to devote more hours to her work and continued to write steadily over the next two years.

In the summer of 1886, another experience helped to stimulate her thoughts and to encourage her in her work. While Robert and his family took a long vacation in Sewanee, Sada was able to leave her mother in the care of family members and get away from the mountain for a time. She traveled to Baltimore to visit friends and to attend the summer classes at Johns Hopkins. Apart from auditing occasional classes with professors at Sewanee, this was to be her only formal university study. Her professor at Johns Hopkins was Dr. James Wilson Bright, an eminent philologist and Shakespearean scholar, a cofounder of *Modern Language Notes*. [48]

Women were not formally admitted as students at Johns Hopkins until the early 1900s, and so no university record has been preserved of Sada's summer study, according to the registrar. However, a social note in a Baltimore paper contained the following item which confirms her pioneering presence: "Miss Elliott, daughter of Bishop Elliott of Georgia, is visiting Mrs. John Cuyler of Baltimore. She is noted for her intellectuality, though she is in no wise pedantic, and is pleasantly known as a charming authoress. She is the first lady to avail herself of the tutelage of the professors of the Johns Hopkins University, and will spend some months in Baltimore for that purpose." [49] Like her father and grandfather, Sada believed in education as a continuing, lifelong experience. Largely self-educated herself, she was a strong advocate of higher education for women as well as men. Indeed, in 1910 she helped formulate a plan for an extension school at the University of the South, part of a new movement nationwide to allow part-time students to upgrade their degrees or simply to enrich their personal lives through university course work in the summer and at home by mail.

Upon returning from Baltimore, Sada found Bishop Elliott's family in great concern over his health. His rapid deterioration was thought to be a result of bouts of malaria and dengue fever, together with the strain of constant travel as a frontier bishop. Doctors urged him to rest and to travel for the restoration of mind and body. Since his great wish had always been to visit the Holy Land, the family scraped together the necessary funds and after much persuasion "bought him out" over his modest protestations. Sada decided to go along with him and help care for the semiinvalid. [50]

Sale of her story "A Simple Heart" to the *Independent* (November 1886) helped Sada pay for her part of the forthcoming trip. This latest coup, having a story published in a large national weekly magazine, gave her the confidence to contract with the *Louisville Courier-Journal* to publish several of her pieces, including a short story laid in Texas called "Mrs. Gollyhaw's Candy-stew," as well as a series of travel sketches she proposed to write from various cities along her route through Europe and the Middle East.

The contract called for thirteen sketches, but the series eventu-

ally stretched to sixteen articles printed at two- to three-week
intervals from November 1886 to August 1887. Payment at ten
dollars for each essay was to be deposited in her brother's account in
a New York bank. Arrangements had been made in Louisville by a
friend, Mrs. Alice B. Castleman. But Mrs. Castleman neglected to
obtain a written agreement for payment, and Sada learned to her
dismay in June 1887 that so far nothing had been paid to the account
for the hundreds of words already published. After she sent several
anxious letters from various parts of the Continent, the promised
funds seem eventually to have been paid.[51]

This financial tangle was but one of a series of setbacks on the
tour. Worst of all, Robert did not rally as the doctors had hoped; in
fact, overexertion in the Egyptian sun, viewing pyramids and
monuments, made him so weak that he had to remain in bed for
several days. Eventually the travelers pushed on from Alexandria,
determined to reach Jerusalem. When they arrived at last, Sada was
totally unprepared for what she found in the Holy City of three
faiths. The weather turned rainy. Her brother's health continued to
deteriorate. On every side she was confronted by poverty and
hunger, and appalled at the commercialization of the holy shrines
she visited. She found herself an "Innocent Abroad" whose eyes
were finally opened to the chicanery of those who prey on unsus-
pecting pilgrims. Some of this feeling of bitter disappointment is
conveyed in a short story entitled "As a Little Child," published in
the *Independent* in December 1887. The story describes a group of
American tourists in Jerusalem, one of whom, an Arkansas
preacher, has his faith deeply shaken by what he sees.

Having reached the Holy Land, Robert decided that he should go
straight home from Jerusalem, for he was unable to eat and was
growing noticeably weaker. Nevertheless, he insisted that Sada stay
to see Italy and visit England, which was to have been the high
point of her trip. He took passage home immediately, arriving in
Savannah in May. His wife, Caroline, took him to Warm Springs,
Virginia, for rest under doctor's care and from there he went on—
against doctor's advice—to attend the general convention of the
Episcopal Church in Chicago. The Elliotts then returned to
Sewanee, where Robert died on August 26, 1887, at the age of forty-
seven years.

Meanwhile, though worried about her brother, Sada stayed on in
Italy most of the late spring and early summer, studying Italian,
writing a great deal, and enjoying occasional side trips with a friend,

Nettie Starkweather. They made a circuit of the Italian pensions, all of which seemed to be filled with impecunious American widows trying to find titled husbands for unattractive daughters. The humor and pathos of this kind of dreary life and the ladies' small pretensions and follies found their way into a short story entitled "A Florentine Idyl." This story and the earlier one about the Holy Land were two of a series of five pieces about Americans abroad published from March 1887 to July 1888 in the *Independent.*

Through Nettie Starkweather Sada was introduced to one expatriate American who would mean a great deal to her in her chosen career as a writer—the author Constance Fenimore Woolson. During the 1880s Woolson published widely acclaimed collections of stories set in the Great Lakes region and the deep South, especially the Carolinas and Florida, and she was enjoying great regard as a local-color writer.[52] She had taken up residence in Europe in 1879, and had lived for extended periods of time in the South. She was thoroughly familiar with the Charleston and Savannah area from which Sada came and had written eloquently of the fallen South in *Rodman the Keeper* (1880). A shy woman, Woolson did not receive many visitors; it must have been an especially generous gesture for her to give welcome to this stranger, an aspiring Southern woman writer eight years her junior.

Though the substance of their conversation is not recorded, the visit was nonetheless an important one for Sada's writing career. Woolson's stories were the kind that Sada knew she herself could write—realistic and focused on development of character. They also dealt with the life of her own beloved South and its people—the mountain cove people, Negroes, the returned veteran, the impoverished gentlewomen—people and events that were part of her daily experience. Most of what Sada had published so far, except for *The Felmeres,* which had no specific regional setting, had been about her Texas travels or her experiences in Europe. From this point on, however, her interest would turn to the South, and her stories as well as her best novel would deal with that section of the nation about which readers were most curious to learn.

In an essay published in 1919 Henry James defined in retrospect the problem of writers of the South when he said that Woolson's stories in *Rodman the Keeper* "have a high value, especially when regarded in the light of the voicelessness of the conquered and reconstructed South. Miss Woolson strikes the reader as having a compassionate sense of this pathetic dumbness having perceived that no social revolution of equal magnitude had ever reflected itself so little in literature, remained so unrecorded, so unpainted and unsung. . . .[53] Although she had not written as a native, Miss Woolson was a sympathetic observer. With objectivity and skilled craftsmanship she had given readers a new understanding of the hardships of the South after 1865. By so doing she had provided a lesson young Southern writers needed.

Though much had been written *about* the South in the 1860s and 1870s by outsiders like DeForest, Tourgée, and Woolson herself, the native writers had been silent. Then with publication of Sidney Lanier's *Tiger-Lilies* (1867) and George Washington Cable's *Grandissimes* (1880) there came a torrent of material by Southerners: the poetry of Timrod, Lanier, and Hayne, followed by the stories of Joel Chandler Harris, Grace King, Sherwood Bonner, Mary Noailles Murfree, and many others. The crest of this new wave brought Mark Twain's achievement in *Life on the Mississippi* (1883). By 1887 local-color material about all parts of the South, by Southerners themselves, filled the national magazines; the South was at last becoming vocal indeed.

Woolson's example and encouragement must have caused Sada to see herself as one of these regional voices. Within months after this crucial meeting in May 1887, Sada was sending her own Southern stories to *Harper's, Scribner's,* and *Lippincott's,* which had published many of Woolson's stories. More important, Arthur Stedman, Woolson's literary agent in New York, also became Sada's agent. In a note of farewell on leaving Florence, Sada commented to Woolson on the importance of her encouragement: "I thank you very much for the welcome you were kind enough to give me, and for the interest you showed in me. I know that in taking writing as my work in life—I have begun a long struggle where nothing but hard work will avail. I hope you will give me your good wishes?"[54]

From Italy, Sada made her way to England, carrying out her intention of traveling to London, Oxford, Warwick Castle, and Stratford. She continued to send travel letters home to the *Courier-Journal* with great regularity, but it must have been difficult for her to keep up the light, humorous tone of these pieces, for, in a set of personal letters written at the same time to her sister Esther, she offers a very different story of the journey, filled with depression and growing alarm about her brother's health.[55] Sada received by cable on August 27 the dreaded news of Robert's death at Sewanee. She took the next ship home, too late to do more than join the mournful family circle.

The seven months of travel and her meeting with Woolson had been another turning point for Sada. Yet, despite her disappointments and anxieties she had been an absorbed traveler. Her travel letters show her to have been alive to every new situation, intensely aware of the past through her study of history, conscious of the incongruities of the present, and intrigued by the endless diversity of humanity.

In the months immediately following her brother's death, Sada tried to occupy herself with efforts to collect material for a biography of the widely admired frontier bishop. She wrote dozens of letters to friends and acquaintances, asking them to send her anecdotes about his college years, his military career, the impressions he made upon various parishioners in Georgia and in New York, where he had served as rector. But responses were disappointing. Most persons, she found, were not keepers of letters and mementos. While there were numerous letters of condolence filled with praise for her brother, there were few of the specific details that she sought.[56] Since there was not enough of substance to flesh out a biography, she reluctantly abandoned the project. Instead, she put her energy into completing a novel called *John Paget*, which would contain many parallels with her brother's life and would illustrate many of his ideas.

At the same time, a more ambitious project was beginning to take shape in these years—a local-color novel using characters from the Cumberland Mountains. After nearly twenty years' residence in these mountains, she had learned to recognize the local habits and reproduce the nuances of speech of the mountain people. Combining this knowledge with information about railroads and mining operations acquired from her brother Habersham, and adding something about the economic theories of the day, she produced *Jerry* (1891), her most popular novel and greatest financial success. It is the story of a mountain child who runs away from a brutal father and is adopted by a backwoods gold miner. Educated by the kindly town physician, he becomes a teacher and labor leader in the community and finally falls heir to the gold miner's secret fortune. Corrupted by wealth, he falters and comes to a tragic end.

The manuscript of *Jerry* was sent first to the *Independent*, but was finally bought by *Scribner's* for serialization. An English professor

friend of Sada's from Virginia, W. Gordon McCabe, took the
manuscript personally to Henry Holt for a reading. Holt was
impressed with the material and, after calling for some revisions,
decided to publish it. The novel ran serially in *Scribner's* from June
1890 through May 1891 and then appeared as a book under Holt's
imprint. *Jerry* was an overnight success. Sarah Barnwell Elliott
found herself suddenly the writer of the hour.

Reviews poured in, and editions appeared in England and Australia; the novel was even translated into German the following year.
Holt offered to reissue *The Felmeres*, already in its second printing
(1886) with D. Appleton & Company, and gave a favorable reading
to *John Paget*, which was issued two years after *Jerry*, in 1893.

An especially welcome accolade following her success with *Jerry*
came from Thomas Nelson Page, dean of Southern writers. His
praise elicited the following modest reply from Sada: "Whatever I
may be in other walks of life and time, in the literary world I am just
cutting my teeth, and the sensation of being able to put away the
'spoon vittles' of uncertain hope and in its place to wrestle with the
tough beef of an unexpected success, is like a water-melon—rather
'filling for the price.' "[57]

Financial success was certainly not unwelcome, either. Her bank
account, which seldom showed more than $100 at a time, would for
once not be a major concern to her. Always a cautious spender, she
complained of being unable to dress as elaborately as those of her
circle; yet she always managed to look ladylike and presentable.
Other small frugalities—like writing on the front and back of pages
and saving scrap paper for notes and rought drafts—allowed her to
eke out her royalties for several financially secure years.

The old log cabin behind the Sewanee house, which Sada had
used as a study, was nicknamed "Jerry" after her now-popular
hero. Here she continued to work on a group of short stories
entirely different from her "travel" sketches with their exotic settings and expatriate American characters. The new stories—spare,
well written, and realistic—were grounded in her own family
experiences and were to form a kind of loose social history of the
deep South from the 1850s onward.

VI   "I Took Possession—of Myself . . ."

About sunset on the last day of the year 1895, a small, neat-
appearing middle-aged woman, not fashionably dressed, climbed

the stairs to the top floor of a rooming house on New York's East 27th Street and entered the rooms she had just rented.

Sada Elliott stood for a while looking over the narrow yard at the back of the house to the rooftops casting odd-shaped shadows in the gathering dusk. Then, arranging her few belongings, she laid out her writing materials on a low table near the window and ate supper from a tray, after which she went out again to attend the Watch Services ushering in the New Year at the Church of the Incarnation not far away.

It must have occurred to Sada as she opened a hard-backed ledger next morning, dated the entry January 1, 1896, and began to write down all that had happened since her arrival in New York, that the scene would make an appropriate beginning of a novel. In a novelette called "Fortune's Vassals" (1899) she would, in fact, use much the same scene of a woman arriving in a strange town to become a writer. She expressed in her journal the significance of this new beginning for her life: "Yesterday I took possession of my own time, of myself."

According to entries in her journal, Sarah Barnwell Elliott was reborn that day, "born to my real self," free of the sad, pinch-penny years full of family responsibililty, of a mind divided between domestic duty and the desire for a full-time career. Never before had the way been completely clear for her to work. She had already published three novels, a series of travel letters, and many short stories, sketches, and reviews. In her trunk lay a number of manuscripts waiting to be reworked. Yet, in spite of this auspicious beginning, she had never before been so free to use her time entirely for writing.

The death of her mother on June 27, 1895, at the age of eighty-five had left Sada truly alone for the first time in her life. The sense of release from responsibility had not yet turned to loneliness. After winding up her mother's affairs, she found herself with a small income from municipal and railway bonds, not quite enough to live on but enough to keep her going until more of her work could be sold.

There were several advantages in a move to New York, not the least of which was the challenge to "make it" on her own as a professional writer. There were other things as well: long afternoon walks to furnish new sensations, new books available at the nearest bookshop, concerts, an occasional play, the opera. According to her journal, one of her first purchases soon after her arrival was a new

edition of the plays of Shakespeare. There were also professional
advantages: publishers and literary agents close at hand, as well as
clubs and writers' groups with whose members one might share
common literary problems and interests. Sada soon joined and
became active in several clubs, including the Women's Press Club,
the Authors' League of America, the Barnard and Wednesday
Afternoon Clubs, and the Woman's Political Union. Sometime later
she was invited to join the Lyceum of London; she was already a
member and became vice-president of the Association of Southern
Writers.[58]

Her exhilaration lasted just three months. Then news of family
illness at home began to arrive. Her brother-in-law, the Reverend
Dr. Francis Shoup, died the following summer. Also, the dark days
of winter and a late spring had their effect on a sun-loving Southern
temperament. Dreary hours spent trying to condense an overlong
novel brought on bouts of depression. Of five sketches she had
recently written, only the shortest had been sold. Despite frequent
warnings from her brother, Sada continued her tendency to overwork.

To supplement her income she had taken a job as writer-compiler
for a compendious history of world literature being edited by
Charles Dudley Warner. Her task involved long hours of reading in
order to turn out five or six short pages of biography and criticism for
the "B" volume of the series—Birrell, Browning, and others. This
hack work left no time or energy for the quality of writing she had
intended to do. Her journal reflected her determination to last out
the year in New York if she could, but more and more it also
reflected doubt and homesickness for "dear Sewanee." Finally, on
March 12, 1896, she wrote, "A journal is too saddening. I shall
desist." What other difficulties she faced in the next months one can
only guess. But she stayed.

When Sada Elliott arrived in New York to "take possession of
herself," she was already forty-seven, an age when most of her
contemporaries were already white-haired grandmothers. At forty-
seven her appearance belied her age. Photographs show her to have
been slim, petite, and gracefully feminine, with large, lustrous eyes
that gave her an expectant "wide-eyed" look of youth. Her hair
would not gray for more than a decade. She boasted that a census
taker had once asked her age and she had blithely subtracted twenty
years without his being the wiser. Her manner too was youthful,
and many of her contemporaries spoke of how she could charm an

entire room with her animated conversation and witty remarks. Always outgoing, she was not long in making a wide circle of friends in New York, with whom she shared dinner and theater engagements. Her address book was amply filled with the names and addresses of New York acquaintances—Chaunceys, Potters, Aldriches, and the E. C. Stedmans, among others.

Youthful in mind and spirit, she kept herself open to new ideas through constant reading. She would remain alert and in good health until her eightieth year. Now more than halfway through her life, she felt she was only beginning. She told herself that life was, after all, a *study* for the dedicated writer, and she determined never to give up studying it. The number and variety of things which interested her actually grew with time rather than diminishing. There were ahead of her major contributions to writing, to education in the South, and to the cause of woman's rights.

In order to publish regularly and profitably, Sada needed a good literary agent. She had found one in Arthur Stedman, son of the poet-editor E. C. Stedman, who handled most of her work during her New York years. Despite occasional statements of displeasure with minor matters, Sada appears to have been satisfied with the arrangements that her literary agent made for her, and found them profitable.[59] During her New York years, 1896-1901, Stedman helped her to place two more novels, a novelette, a biography of Sam Houston, seventeen short articles and stories, and a short-story collection. She worked steadily and well, and many of her original hopes for a literary career were realized.

Not all of her time was spent at her writing table, however: as her reputation grew, there were many invitations and pleasant diversions, mentioned in her frequent letters to her brother Hab, who now managed her business affairs. She wrote to him from places with exotic names, from summer homes of friends on Long Island and in Maine and Canada. In the winter there were meetings of clubs, theater, lectures. At the end of one 1898 letter Sada wrote her brother of her pleasure at being so much "in the thick of things." While visiting her friend Mrs. Elihu Chauncey in York Harbor, Maine, that summer, she had met at tea some of the great names in American letters of her day: William Dean Howells; Thomas Nelson Page, with whom she had long been acquainted; Henry W. Van Dyke; and she added with satisfaction that "Mr. [Charles Dudley] Warner will be joining our little summer colony soon."[60]

That same year, along with the rest of the nation, she seems to

have been caught up in "remember the Maine" fever. She even
went so far as to persuade S. S. McClure to send her to Cuba as a
war correspondent. She knew Cuba at second hand from trips made
there by her father and other relatives and from connections by
marriage with her cousins the Gonzaleses of South Carolina. She
wrote to Hab that *McClure's* was willing to send her—so willing that
the firm paid her way to Richmond to see General Fitzhugh Lee to
ask him to arrange transportation for her. Lee was unable to promise
her anything, since he had no power and was unsure if he himself
would go. The adventure fell through.[61]

One result of Sada's interest in the Cuban affair was a short story
entitled "Hands All Round" (*Book News*, September 1898), about
recruitment of Southerners to fight along with other citizens in the
Spanish-American War. The story reflected the vast change in race
relations that had taken place in the South since the end of Reconstruction.

Her work was being sought after more and more. The editors of
the *Outlook* commissioned her to write an essay to be published in
the first issue of the new year, January 1901, summarizing the
changes in literature in the century just ended. She gave it the title
"The Spirit of the Nineteenth Century in Fiction." At the same
time, she was attempting something entirely new, a romantic play
about the English Cavaliers, *His Majesty's Servant*, her first venture
in writing for the theater. The plot centers on the adventures of
Mohun, a stage player thrown out of work by the closing of the
theaters during the Puritan interregnum in 1651. Mohun is loyal to
the exiled King Charles and has the opportunity at the climax of the
play to save the king's life. The play was originally copyrighted in
1902 with "Maud Hosford" as coauthor, although it is not clear who
Miss Hosford was—aside from the fact that she once published a
volume of poetry—or what contribution she made to the play. The
original draft and subsequent emendations are made in Sada's
handwriting. Sada's choice of subject for the play may be explained
in part by her reading of English history and her fondness for British
authors. A niece, Mrs. Charles McD. Puckette, noted in a letter
that her aunt "was a great Anglophile and thought our revolution
was a great mistake—we should still be an English colony."[62]
Nowhere is this sentiment better shown than in her play.

Sada's script was read and accepted by a British theatrical company directed by Lewis Waller. The production opened at the

Imperial Theater, London, on October 6, 1904, and ran successfully
for 100 performances. Sada's nephew R. W. B. Elliott was in
London for the opening-night performance and the next day cabled
his aunt: "Herald says play successfully produced. Distinct Theatrical Success. Congratulations."[63] Among Sada's papers are copies of
two other plays which were never published: a four-act play entitled
"The Widow Neville," carrying the pseudonym "E. B. Sull" as
author, apparently written for drama competition; and a short
one-act play entitled "Moonshine Whiskey." While these two products of Sada's pen show something about her methods of composition, they add little of value to the body of her work.

A novelette, "Fortune's Vassals" (*Lippincott's*, August 1899), and a
novel, *The Making of Jane* (1901) were also products of Sada's New
York years. The acceptance of both for publication was aided by
Arthur Stedman. The subject of the novelette—independence for
women—reflected Sada's growing commitment to the woman's
rights movement. "Fortune's Vassals" makes an argument for recognition of "the new woman" as a professional with her own work and
freedom to pursue her own destiny, separate from her husband and
not totally subject to his will. *The Making of Jane*, which was to be
the last major piece Sada would publish, is the full-length portrait of
a young woman struggling for independence both from ties of family
obligation and from the shallow life of a socialite whose only role in
life is that of a "prize" in the marriage game. This portrait of "the
new woman" paralleled Sada's own struggles for professional status.
It was a fitting capstone to her independent New York years.

VII   *Return to Sewanee*

Perhaps Sada might have produced other novels and other theatrical successes like *His Majesty's Servant* if she had continued to live
and work in New York; but by 1902 she was tired and discouraged.
Popular tastes had changed, and there was very little market now for
local-color material. In 1901, upon returning to New York after a
quiet summer at Sewanee, she had expressed doubts to Hab about
her next course of action: "My plans are still uncertain, depending
on what I can make, but my wish is to return to Sewanee as soon as
possible. To save my life I cannot say what is the wise thing to do—I
can live more cheaply at Sewanee but I have more leisure for work
in New York, and more stimulus. There is nothing stimulating at

Sewanee—not to be conceited, I have outgrown it. I ought to be sufficient to myself . . . the wretched thought came to me that I was obliged to keep the pot boiling—wretched pot."[64]

Soon afterward, her decision was made for her. Illness and adversity had plagued the life of "Dawtie," Sada's younger sister, and in 1901 she had finally come home to Sewanee to live, bringing with her her three young sons. In 1902 Dawtie died after a lingering illness. Two years later her husband also died, leaving the three boys orphaned. They became the legal wards of Sada Elliott.

Suddenly at fifty-four Sada had a new role to perform—adoptive parent to her three half-grown nephews. It seemed as though her life kept following a script she had already, almost prophetically, written for it. In both *Jerry* and in *The Making of Jane* she had explored the problems of orphaned or impoverished children being reared by others. Now she was faced with the same problem in her own life.

Sada felt that she had a moral obligation to make a real home for her nephews, to see them through their schooling, and to help each one become established in an occupation. In 1904 she made her removal from New York to Sewanee permanent, although she visited New York occasionally with friends and relatives to take care of business matters and to enjoy a sampling of plays, the opera, and the symphony. The independent years were over.

In the nine years which followed, she succeeded in helping "her boys," Stephen, Charles, and John Puckette, finish college at the University of the South and make a start in the work world. Stephen, the eldest, with the help of his Uncle Habersham, became a civil engineer. The second boy, Charles, became a member of the staff of the *New York Evening Post,* moving eventually to the staff of *The New York Times* and finally becoming managing editor of a *Times* subsidiary, the *Chattanooga Times* in Tennessee. John, the third boy, also went into newspaper work, and eventually publishing.

Once her nephews were well launched, Sada was able to travel again. In 1907, twenty years after her first visit to Europe, she again went abroad, visiting places she had missed on her earlier, ill-fated journey with her ailing brother. She spent the winter of 1907-1908 in Rome, her favorite of southern European cities.

Better known in New York and London than in her home state of Tennessee, Sada Elliott outlined her writing career in an interview published in the *Nashville Tennessean* on September 29, 1907.

After listing her major writings, she described her method of composition in this way:

Sometimes I am asked whether or not I plan a story and outline the plot before beginning to write, or again whether I gather materials in the way of events or character studies from the life around me. I do neither. The genesis of a story in my mind comes from my interest in some type of character or some problem of human life. Then I try to work this out in narrative form. I do not plan the end of the story from the beginning, nor the full development of characters from the first. My characters, in a sense, develop themselves and the story evolves itself.

Sometimes I spend weeks or months without writing at all. I do not try to force myself to regular hours of work, even when I am writing—my life is so irregular that I could not. When I do write, I write continuously on one book—I do not try to carry on two or three at a time.

Between 1901 and 1907, except for her play and a couple of book reviews for the *Sewanee Review,* she published only eight short pieces of fiction. Half of these were for children and were published in the *Youth's Companion,* a popular magazine which paid well but promised no new luster for her career.

Soon after her return from Europe in 1908, she became engrossed in the problems and possibilities of the changing New South. The national trend toward extending educational opportunities to all, especially to women, suggested the idea for establishing some kind of extension program at the University of the South. A summer conference on problems of the New South, held at Sewanee, produced some papers of more than casual interest. These were published in a new quarterly directed at a growing readership among the politically concerned Southern middle class. Sada not only wrote for the new quarterly, the *Forensic Quarterly Review,* but helped edit its last two issues.

For all its visionary fervor, the *Forensic Quarterly* found a cool reception for its papers on such highly controversial issues as labor relations, racial injustice, and woman's rights, and it lasted less than two years (1910-1911). By then Sada was deeply involved in woman's suffrage activities in Tennessee and probably spent little time lamenting the close of her brief editorial activities.

Through membership in the Woman's Political Union of New York, Sada had begun to take an active part in the work of bringing about equal suffrage. This participation intensified after her move back to Tennessee, especially with the formation of the statewide

Tennessee Equal Suffrage Association, made up of active local suffrage groups in Chattanooga, Nashville, and other cities. On January 5, 1911, Sada returned to New York to deliver a lecture entitled "A Sketch of the History of the Woman Suffrage Movement in the United States" for the Equal Franchise Society. Although the text of her lecture has not been preserved, the title alone suggests the breadth of her knowledge about the suffrage movement.[65]

Because of her long association with woman's rights and suffrage issues, her abilities as a public speaker, and also because of her 1901 novel on the new woman, *The Making of Jane*, Sada was a logical choice to head the work of woman's suffrage in her home state. In January 1912 at the annual meeting in Nashville she was chosen president of the Tennessee Equal Suffrage Association. Numerous speaking engagements took her from Alabama to Illinois that year, and she also wrote and distributed in behalf of the association a ringing "Manifesto," a strongly worded petition for the right to vote, which was published in the *Nashville Banner* on August 17, 1912.[66]

Sada was re-elected president of the Tennessee Association in 1913. Meanwhile she had also been serving as vice-president of the Southern States Woman Suffrage Conference. This regional post brought her in touch with suffrage activists from neighboring Southern states, women like Laura Clay of Kentucky, and fellow novelist Mary Johnston of Virginia. Jointly these three requested to appear before the Tennessee legislature. The request was granted and Sarah Barnwell Elliott became the first woman to address that legislative body.[67] Another activity of this eventful year was a nationally organized march on Washington in which Sada took part.[68]

Sada Elliott was responsible for inviting the National American Woman Suffrage Association to hold its annual meeting in Tennessee in 1914, a strategy designed to focus national attention on the South. All eyes were now on Tennessee, for as yet no Southern state had ratified the Nineteenth Amendment, and at least one more state vote was needed if the amendment were to become law. But an unfortunate and petty dispute arose among the members of the Tennessee Association over the site for the national meeting. This resulted in a split in the ranks of the organization. At this point Sada resigned due to "ill health," actually suffering from strain and overwork. "I am not meant for this sort of thing—I so long to stay in my little study and do my own little work—ponder on my own little problems and evolve my own little stories. It has been a long time since I could do these pleasant things," she confessed to the poet Wallace Rice, a friend, in January 1913.[69]

The controversy was resolved in favor of Nashville and the national meeting took place as scheduled in November 1914, bringing national and international speakers to the state capital. This all-important meeting constituted a turning point leading to eventual ratification. However, in spite of the untold effort on the part of various women's organizations, the suffrage debate dragged on until 1920, when the constitutional amendment was at last ratified by the Tennessee legislature by a very narrow margin. Even after passage the vote was contested for several days by the well-organized antisuffrage faction. The ratification was eventually validated, however, and with it Tennessee became the thirty-sixth and crucial state to ratify, making the Nineteenth Amendment the law of the land.

While the long fight was going on, Sada had also accepted the invitation to lend her name and influence to the Democratic Wilson-Marshall ticket. "Accepted with joy—and worked," she wrote on the telegram of invitation.[70] As chairman of the state women's committee she wrote letters, distributed literature, and raised money. On election day 1912 she experienced the extreme gratification of seeing her party and candidate victorious.

Wilson's election seemed a special personal victory for Sada. He was in every respect the ideal candidate: an aristocratic Southerner by birth, an educator, possessing an interest in history and an intellectual's approach to solving contemporary problems. In the next eight years the Wilson administration confirmed her every expectation in the area of domestic legislation, carrying into law not only the Nineteenth Amendment but also child labor laws and voting reforms, issues which were part of the woman's rights cause.

In recognition of her intense efforts in behalf of woman's suffrage and her now well established reputation as a writer, Sada Elliott was awarded the degree of Doctor of Civil Law, Honoris Causa, by the University of the South on Commencement Day, June 17, 1913. The degree was a source of great pride to her.

With the return to power of the Republicans in 1920, politics lost much of its savor for Sada. To her there could never be another era quite like the triumphant Wilson years. Clippings among her papers attest to her close interest in Wilson's career, which she had followed since he was a student at Johns Hopkins while she was there in 1886. She was especially proud of his work in forming the League of Nations, and she fretted over every word from his critics.

But with Harding in the White House she could only comment acidly, "Nobody could be a greater failure than poor old Harding—memorialized by a black two-cent stamp!"[71] In the privacy of another letter to Hab she vented her often caustic wit upon Harding's successor as well: "Coolidge," she commented, "reminds me of a flaxseed poultice—Mother used to put them on us, you remember—also flaxseed tea—it was not wholly bad—but slimy."[72]

The 1920s found Sada living quietly at Sewanee, still reading widely and doing a small amount of writing, though publishing little. She looked forward to visits from her young nieces and nephews and wrote them delightful, fanciful letters full of stories and make-believe, which were tucked away as family treasures. She loved to hear of the young people's accomplishments and maintained a vast correspondence, relaying messages for all branches of her large family. She was delighted when Huger Elliott, a nephew, was named head of the education department of the Metropolitan Museum of Art in New York. Hab's daughter Hannah had also become an artist and was receiving portrait commissions from many parts of the country. Sada once commented wryly that she wished Hannah could receive a commission to paint President Coolidge, for "though it might ruin her sense of the beautiful, it would at least give her something to buy the beautiful with."

Sada wrote a few pieces about Sewanee life during these years and once delivered a long humorous speech in verse about the "E.Q.B." [Ecce quam bonum] Society, a social and literary group, founded in 1870, which held dinner meetings at least once a year at Sewanee. After her sister Esther's death in 1916, she carried on the work of the Henneman Club in support of the University Library. She also collected family reminiscences and genealogy studies of her pioneer forebears and maintained her affiliation with the Daughters of the Confederacy, the Historical Society of South Carolina, and the Colonial Dames.

In these last years she wrote several book reviews for the Sewanee Review which reveal the scope of her reading. Her review of Howard Odum's Southern Pioneers (1925) sadly concurred with his analysis of the failure of the New South to produce leaders as it had in earlier times: the failure to make quick adjustment to social change; the lack of experience and training for new leadership; lack of universities; lack of an atmosphere conducive to achievement and distinction; lack of recognition of merit within her own borders.[73] Every statement was true, she admitted, even making allowances for the devastation suffered by the South during the Civil War. The intellectual—and the writer, she might have added—had been a prophet without honor in the South.

Since 1870 Sada had been a well-known and much-beloved figure at Sewanee. For nearly half a century the Elliott house had been a center of social life where one could always find a stimulating conversation on Sunday afternoon. Sada continued her mother's practice of keeping "open house" for visitors one afternoon a week, and her Mondays were invariably attended by students, faculty, and friends. She was something of an "official hostess" and always housed, fed, and entertained visiting guest speakers at the university, such as the poet Wallace Rice and the writer Ruth McEnery Stuart.

She presented a familiar figure, often dressed in cool (and economical) white—also symbolically worn by Suffragettes in their marches. Her hair was bobbed in the latest fashion of the 1920s, giving her a youthful appearance which belied her seventy or more years. She was as much a "fixture" at Sewanee as the chapel services and her habits were as unvarying as the university fraternity rituals.[74] For example, her nephew Stephen recalled how she had trained her two English setters, Rob and Hab, who followed her everywhere, to stop and wait for her at the gate until she returned from church services. Her signal to them was to hold up her prayer book to indicate where she was going. Even when she went to visit friends or attend a card party, it was said that she always carried her prayer book with her as a sign to her pets that they must not follow her.[75]

With age, Sada had retained her clear mind and pungent wit, along with a healthy skepticism and sense of irony. From her novels one receives the impression that despite her outward cheerfulness she viewed life as essentially tragic, filled with tremendous ironies. This attitude seems not to have evolved with the years but to have been present all along in the visionary, deeply religious examiner of self and others. She had looked out across a tumultuous past and had worked hopefully for a more promising future for her sex and for her region. The wide gulf between her hopes and their full realization was a sobering part of her awareness.

And yet some of her hopes *had* been realized and she could count successes in many areas that had been important to her. She felt the North had come to have a better understanding of the devastated South and the mistakes of Reconstruction. Both sections had also come to share a better awareness of the problems of the Negro following emancipation. Members of her sex had won the legal battles they had fought for, if not all the economic and political status they sought. Her own work had provided her an intellectual outlet and a modest livelihood. Her boys had reached maturity, completed their education, and become well established on their own. Her beloved Sewanee, despite financial setbacks, had continued to grow and enhance its scholastic reputation in the South and in the nation.

She had learned to live with loneliness in the silent life of her own emotions. Her outward accomplishments had earned her an honorary degree and a place in *Who's Who in America*. Not only had she not disgraced her family—as she feared at eighteen she might do by publishing unwisely or too soon—she had instead added new luster to an already illustrious name.

When death came from cancer on August 30, 1928, Sada Elliott in her eightieth year was still looking to the future, awaiting publication of a story entitled "The Infinite Wrong," which had been tentatively accepted by the editor of the *Manchester Guardian*.

CHAPTER 2

Apprenticeship

I *Premises*

SARAH Elliott was destined to wander wide afield before finding her true path as a writer. Her earliest pieces, apart from the somber religious and woman's rights themes of her first novel, lack a strong sense of purpose and direction. She tried a variety of topics and narrative ideas, drawing an occasional interesting characterization, but her plots were weak and barely escaped sentimentality. Gradually, however, she found her way into local color and moved toward themes that would interest a national rather than a regional audience.

Succeeding chapters in this study will trace her steps as she moved from apprenticeship to the major themes that occupied Americans in the last quarter of the nineteenth century. From her first trial pieces about the frontier West, she turned to depicting the impact of older European culture on Americans abroad on the Continent. She drew upon her own travel experiences and obviously was influenced by Twain's *Innocents Abroad*. As her experience broadened, and with the encouragement and advice of Constance Fenimore Woolson, she returned to write about her native region with new eyes. Gradually she became involved in the problems of the New South emerging from the throes of Radical Reconstruction into a period of industrialization, populist politics, and finally the woman's rights movement.

Concomitant with this search for significant themes was a search for a style best suited to her own identity and writer's purpose. Loyal to the South, yet no romantic seeking to relive the antebellum life, she struggled to present her view of the region to a nation of readers preconditioned to view it with suspicion if not hostility. She knew the impossibility of writing for her own circle; the bankrupt and impoverished South had never been, and was not about to become, a book-buying region. To succeed financially she knew she had to appeal to a national audience. The newly emerging techniques of Realism served her in this effort, though she was never able to rid her writing totally of vestiges of the sentimentalism found in much popular fiction of the period.

A detailed look at her work requires a survey of the themes found in her writings, and a description of the ways in which she drew upon Realism to achieve her distinctive style and serve her point of view. Her stories and novels touch upon many themes common to writers in the United States in the second half of the nineteenth century. She writes of industrialization and its effect on the quality of human life. She is especially concerned with the impact on the post-Civil War agrarian South as it moves into mercantile and industrial enterprises for the first time. Well aware that urbanization and industrial "wage slavery" had had their effect elsewhere, she has one of her characters in the novel *John Paget* go to work in the New York slums among victims of poverty and despair. *Jerry* explores the abuses of expansionism and railroad and land fraud and offers collective ownership as a solution to the economic woes of the mine workers in the story. In numerous stories and novels she ponders the quarrel between science and religion and the decline of religious orthodoxy. The effects of rapid change, so often reiterated by other writers, are seen in her work, especially in those stories dealing with the dislocations of an entire society in the South after the war. The changing role of women figures prominently in several stories and novels. These themes make her work not so much original as representative of the social and moral concerns of an age. They show her to have been alive to the leading issues of her time and eager to address the struggle for social justice. But, though searching out representative themes, Elliott retained a Southern point of view that inevitably dominates and, in some ways, limits her perspective.

C. Vann Woodward, in *The Burden of Southern History* (1968), has explored this Southern point of view, a sense of unique identity, and especially a view of the past, which may be distinguished from that of other regions or of the nation as a whole. What is uniquely Southern, he feels, is an awareness of failure, an experience not shared by any part of the nation. In "The Search for Southern Identity" he describes the collective Southern experience as one of failure and frustration, a knowledge of poverty and a sense of guilt, resulting in a view of life that is both tragic and ironic.[1] In contrast,

Puritan New England, he feels, tended from the beginning toward an optimistic viewpoint; the American continent was seen as a New Eden and the American as a New Adam, and the entire American experience was to be an opportunity for a return to innocence. (F. O. Matthiessen, R. W. B. Lewis, and others have used similar insights for many years as a way to interpret some of the themes that recur in our national literature.[2])

The South, on the other hand, has grown up with a sense of guilt rather than a sense of innocence. The burden of slavery, the reality of war and of defeat, and afterward fifty years of regional poverty and political corruption have made the South's story far different from the typical American success story. The South has known frustration and defeat. "It had learned what it was to be faced with economic, social, and political problems that refused to yield to all the in-genuity, patience, and intelligence that a people could bring to bear upon them."[3] In sum, Woodward feels that the South was forced to grasp the implication of evil, the loss of innocence, long before the rest of the nation, and that it has had to come to grips with these sobering realities.

The Southern point of view, then, is tragic and ironic, the two qualities which tend to dominate the work of recent Southern writers, especially Faulkner. In the last three decades, the South's literary renaissance has been filled with great themes arising from its historical consciousness. Confirms Woodward: "The themes that have inspired the major writers have not been the flattering myths nor the romantic dreams of the South's past . . . they have turned instead to the somber realities of hardship and defeat and evil and 'the problems of the human heart in conflict with itself.' "[4]

This turning to the realities of hardship and to themes of the heart in conflict with itself can be seen clearly emerging in the work of Sarah Barnwell Elliott half a century earlier. By her direct experi-ence with slavery and the war, the economic deprivation and anxiety of Reconstruction, and the emerging struggles for legal status by blacks and by women she was thrust into the midst of this regional dilemma. She attempted to achieve some sort of detach-ment from these problems by her removal to New York City, hoping to become better able to understand and describe them and to abstract universal meaning from them. But her eventual return suggests that in the end personal ties and her own "heart in conflict with itself" overcame intellectual detachment.

Her fictional forays through the region she loved do not take her beyond the boundaries of her own experience, and her conclusions about many issues are often ambivalent. As she looked at the question of honor, for example, she saw in it both good and evil. Honor sustains Helen Felmere, heroine of her first novel, through a bad marriage, but it also drives her to self-destruction. Unreasoning adherence to the code of honor also drives sons and brothers to fight useless duels and costs the lives of good men, in fiction as in real life.

In the area of race relations Elliott sees the depths of the problem but stops short of facing up to much-needed reforms. She can poke a satiric finger at the paternalism of Miss Maria and can also admire the generosity of Kizzy, her former slave, who in one story goes to work to support her former mistress. She can portray the ferocity of a lynch mob but cannot bring herself to speak out forcefully in behalf of white responsibility to provide education and equal status for the black man. In some ways she successfully presents a nonromantic, multifaceted view of the collective Southern experience, but in other ways she refrains from the type of candor George Washington Cable displays in *The Negro Question* (1888).

In two aspects of her writing Sarah Elliott differs from the New England regionalists: in their attitudes toward the past and toward childhood. The New England regionalists are often nostalgic for the past, celebrating its vestigial elements in the present. They exalt innocence, in childhood and in nature, in the village, in a simpler style of life that rejects the materialism of the age and the rapid changes wrought by technology. Elliott does not seek to relive the past, although she allows some nostalgic utterances to escape the lips of her characters as she inveighs against materialism. Her stories deal most often with the very recent past or the contemporary scene of the 1880s to 1900s. The stories laid in the postwar era depict—sometimes with humor, sometimes with pathos—the disillusionment, poverty, and despair in the lives of a war-ravaged people and the strategies they evolved for psychic survival. She felt that one carries the past with him, its good and bad traditions, its inherited ideals and beliefs, in the very chemistry of the mind and emotions. The past is seen in terms of heredity, of attitudes and influences passed down from generation to generation. For this reason, she often uses perennial flowers and flowering bulbs as symbols for living links with the past.

She seldom tries to stabilize the present or return to the past. In one story, "The Wreck," the Southern past is symbolized by a wrecked railway engine, a useless relic which lies rusting in a field where children of a postwar generation come to play. The futility of rehearsing the old, sad scenes of war is illustrated in "Jim's Victory" as the daily pantomime of a demented war veteran.

Childhood is not depicted as idyllic or innocent. The young lives of Elliott's heroes and heroines in all her major novels are as disrupted, lonely, and troubled as her own early life had been.

In both novels and stories Elliott chose the new Realism of George Eliot, and of Flaubert and Zola across the Atlantic, in order to avoid lapsing totally into sentimentality. The style involved objectivity, reportorial detachment, use of dialogue, saying much with a few significant details. By describing the words and actions of characters and avoiding lengthy explanations, the Realist enlists the cooperation of the reader's imagination. Short sentences and paragraphs, a minimal preoccupation with painting a picturesque scene, and concentration on revealing character are all aspects of this style.

The purpose of such devices for "representing commonplace things" had nothing less lofty than Truth as their aim, as George Eliot had explained in *Adam Bede*. The technique of photography known as the daguerreotype was often mentioned by writers of this period. It is interesting to observe that several of Elliott's stories actually begin as though they are still photographs that come to life. She uses a magic-lantern technique, with scenes that begin in the middle of the action and flash back to what has gone before. The writer strives for the verisimilitude of the photograph.

II   "Literary Sectionalism . . . Provincial and Stupid"

Though her stories soon were published in the leading national periodicals, Elliott's hard-won perfection of a Realistic style gained her very few readers at home. Southern taste had undergone what a psychiatrist might term a kind of emotional abreaction in the decades following the end of Radical Reconstruction. Readers there seemed to crave the nostalgic and elegiac in their literary fare, the very antithesis of Elliott's Realistic and ironic tone. This apparent rejection at home may have been part of what impelled her to leave her safe mountain precincts for the dangers and follies of New York.

The move to New York in 1895 represented not only her personal declaration of independence but also a break with sectionalism. Elliott felt that in New York she was entering the mainstream of American intellectual life. Henceforth she might write about the

South, but not because of it. Though the South was her locale of choice, she made no special pleading to be published because she was an impoverished Southern gentlewoman who must write or starve. She was all too familiar with those desperate young Southern women like Sherwood Bonner and Mary Noailles Murfree who had had to turn to writing for a livelihood literally to survive.

Elliott made clear her position with regard to sectionalism in a review published the year before she came to New York. Her occasion is the newest collection of poems by the then popular and much sought after Virginia poet John Bannister Tabb, who had built a small reputation on his religious verse and was sometimes compared to Poe. Sada found that the book contained "too little verse and too much paper" to suit her. Of Father Tabb as a distinctly *Southern* poet and of sectionalism in general she says:

> However sectionalism may be allowed to enter into politics and finance, into literature, where such a feeling would combine for us Southerners the evils of both the historical and personal estimates [in criticism], it should not come.
>
> Political sectionalism has caused great trouble; financial sectionalism is causing great trouble; literary sectionalism, if not so troublesome, is to say the least, provincial and stupid.
>
> It is only of late years that the South has allowed sectional feeling to enter her estimate of her own literary work. It used to be said by other parts of the country that the South did not so much as encourage her writers; that they had to go North for acknowledgment and an audience. The answer was that the South held by the highest standards, the "real estimate," and that as not only no Southerner, but no American had touched that high point, the South saw no reason why she should abandon the best and come down to the mediocre simply because it was American. It was right, this "real estimate," but the discouragement of the native literature which would have, and which now has, grown into something, was a serious mistake. . . . But that the sectional or personal estimate should now be allowed to enter into our judgment of literature, is the gravest mistake that can possibly be made, if we may draw conclusions from the indiscriminate praise which Southern papers and people are lavishing upon the small volume before us.[5]

Undoubtedly she had been forming the idea that she wanted to be judged by the "real estimate" of her own work, as an American, not as a primarily Southern writer. Perhaps, too, like Virginia Beaufort in De Forest's *The Bloody Chasm*, she had simply outgrown the need to weep over "the lost cause" or to dwell upon the past, as so many had done, to the exclusion of all else. Like George Washington Cable, she believed that any worthwhile contribution she might make must be toward a national literature.

Elliott was echoing Cable's call to put aside sectionalism in the name of freedom to express the universals of experience, answering also Emerson's call for a *national* literature which would combine the distinctive features of many religions and types within the great American melting pot.

III   The Felmeres

The idea for Elliott's first novel, if not some of the chapters themselves, must have been formed by the time she moved to Sewanee in 1870 and wrote to her brother of having few choices this side of "saint or woman's rights." For it is precisely these two themes which dominate *The Felmeres*. There is very little that could be termed local-color about this darkly Gothic tale which appeared on the booksellers' shelves in the summer of 1879.

From the outset the author was compared with George Eliot, perhaps partly because of their similar last names but more because both were Realistic writers and both were women. The heroine of *The Felmeres* even bears a certain likeness to Dorothea of *Middlemarch* (1871). Helen Felmere is a strong-minded young woman with "ideals" and the desire for a life of greater meaning and depth than that of a housewife. George Eliot's heroine Dorothea marries unhappily; the elderly Cassaubon, her husband, proves to be a dull and exploiting pedant. She later learns to love a young man who is interested in art, and undergoes a period of dejection and reexamination. Helen Felmere, too, marries unhappily and later meets a young artist with whom she falls in love. She suffers long periods of dejection and despair over her religious beliefs. Both women characters, like the authors who created them, represent "new women" who view themselves as separated from the traditional roles of wife and mother. The comparison between her work and Eliot's was flattering to Sada, who had read and had no doubt been influenced by *Middlemarch:* Sada evidently admired all of George Eliot's work, for she collected reviews of Eliot's writings for her scrapbook.

Helen Felmere's story is that of a girl educated by her father to be an atheist like himself. When she grows up, Helen learns that her Roman Catholic mother has separated from her father because of religious differences, taking Helen's only brother with her to be reared a Catholic. Helen worships her father and therefore rejects Christianity together with the mother who has cruelly abandoned her. She vows to follow her father's wise but nonreligious teachings all her life and to share his fate after death.

She is wooed and wed by a cousin, Philip Felmere, who marries her in spite of her unbelief because she is an heiress and because he assumes that, being womanlike, she has no serious convictions and will soon give over her atheistic beliefs. Her father encourages the match, knowing that she will be protected when he dies. Helen agrees to marry, purely as a family alliance and to comply with her father's wishes, but refuses to live with Philip as his wife while her father lives.

Before her cousin-husband comes to claim her six years later, she meets and learns to love a young artist, Felix Gordon, who stays with the family for a summer. Realizing her mistake in marrying her cousin, but unable to go back on her word, Helen sends her artist-suitor away.

A new life begins for her in New York after her father's death. The high-society Felmere relatives, all nominal Christians, are depicted as religious hypocrites. Although Helen cannot believe in Christianity, she has great respect for its ethical teachings and soon sees how far short of ideal Christians her relatives are. They display far less charity and forbearance toward her than she toward them. Rejected more and more by her in-laws, she has only one friend to whom she may turn, and through this friend she is introduced once again to the former suitor, who has moved his artist's studio to the city. Struggling between love and duty, Helen is on the point of suicide when she is prevented from drowning herself by a mysterious clergyman who appears opportunely on the scene.

But now at issue is the fate of her infant son, who will be taken from her by her husband and his family to be brought up according to their faith. Legally, as a woman of the 1870s, she has no right to determine her own child's future. Her in-laws are prepared to have her declared legally unfit to rear him. Helen finally seeks out the only counselor she feels she can trust, the mysterious clergyman who has saved her life. By novelistic coincidence, he is revealed to be her long-lost brother. Unlike other Christians she has met, he seems an honest practitioner of his faith; she is temporarily won over by his persuasive arguments and Christlike life and consents to have her child baptized and reared as a Christian. But at the decisive moment of her child's being taken away, her mother's instinct causes her to rush after him, and she is crushed under a moving carriage. She retains her unbelief to the end, but dies knowing that her brother will protect her child.

The reader becomes interested in Helen and feels sympathetic toward her from the outset. She is depicted as beautiful and intelligent, but also as too painfully honest. Her unbending sense of honor never lets her go back on her word, and it sustains her more than all her philosophical unbelief.

Elliott infuses scenes with a strong pictorial sense. Colors are somber, like Helen's gloomy paintings. The opening scene is a still photograph, or a flat landscape painted upon canvas. At first nothing moves. Then the scene is given depth and brought to life with the wheeling flight of small birds high in the sky and a gradual awareness of the river's motion as it rolls to the sea. The reader's view is that of the author, gazing out into the vast, lonely distances of marsh, sea, and sky—the favorite landscape of Elliott's imagination. The locale of the novel is not named, but one easily recognizes it as typical coastal Georgia and South Carolina—most likely the Port Royal area stretching north into St. Helena Sound above Beaufort and southward to Savannah. This setting, used in the opening scene of the book and again several times throughout, emphasizes the central character's lonely struggle, wandering symbolically in a kind of wasteland between her roles as wife and mother, between tradition and change, between the real and the ideal. Whenever Helen Felmere is made to face a momentous choice, the author places her in this seaside environment. There she contemplates, like Matthew Arnold, the dark tides of doubt from the once-bright shore of faith. The abandonment of orthodoxy, the age of scientific rationalism, and the rebirth of faith as a little child are symbolized as much by setting as by events.

A great deal of the novel seems to be autobiographical: the child Helen is pictured in the opening scenes as "a child, unchildish and over-thoughtful, a lonely little figure on the wide green waste."[6] Brought up in a remote village, leading a lonely and monotonous life, Helen has only her books and her sketching to amuse her. "Sketching" in Elliott's case was her writing—creating her own fantasy world of fictional heroes and fabricated emotions.

Like Elliott, Helen is deeply and loyally attached to her father, whom she thinks of as King Arthur, the noble, righteous, and upright subject of Felix Gordon's portrait. Loyalty to her father's teachings is crucial to Helen's subsequent behavior, just as Elliott herself had tried to emulate her father through study and mastery of self-expression. Even the lost brother, the only true Christian in *The Felmeres,* had a real-life counterpart in Sada Elliott's brother Robert, whose gentle Christian apologetics had had an effect on everyone who heard him.

The cousin-suitor in the novel may also have had a counterpart in Elliott's personal life, for at the time she wrote to Louisa Arnold of "the great disappointment," she had several times mentioned a male cousin who may have courted her.[7] Having decided to remain single, Elliott in her writing shows ambivalence toward marriage; she pictures the marriage of Helen Felmere as hollow and un-fulfilling, a betrothal that is not consummated for an incredibly long period of six years.

More interesting to the reader than these autobiographical parallels, however, are the dialogues between father and daughter on the role of women, on faith, and on the value of Christianity which take place in the earlier parts of the story. When Helen expresses the view that her future mother-in-law is a hypocrite, Hector cautions her that she must learn to accept the failings of others along with the many unavoidable ills of life:

"You must not despise the stupid nor those who find interest in trifles. I tell you there is much wisdom in being able to lose one's self in small pleasures. True wisdom and happiness lie in adapting yourself to whatever state of life you may be driven to fill; else you will always be tearing yourself against the corners of other people's prejudices; and making your existence a burden. Another good rule is to keep your opinions to yourself until they are asked for, then announce them as mildly as you can. Above all, be polite to fools, for they are the most dangerous enemies." (56)

How painfully Elliott had learned to keep her own opinions to herself, having lost a valued friend by just such a mistake. An older, wiser author now offers a Greek philosophic calm, the Stoicism of which Helen and her father are personifications, as a high plateau from which to view the world and its petty emotions. Helen tells her father that she doubts this calm is possible for a woman, a creature of the emotions, who—her future husband tells her—is a "lower animal." "So some men think," Hector replies, "but I cannot see why. Your mind is surely equal to Philip's. But show it—prove it by your very quiet" (58).

Elliott is struggling with arguments about the nature and ability of woman such as those advanced by Mary Wollstonecraft a half century earlier: how can an intelligent woman survive in a society which says she has an immortal soul but an inferior mind and no basic human rights, made subservient to every male relative and treated in legal matters like a slave or imbecile child?[8] What appears on the surface to be primarily a religious novel becomes a vehicle for discussion of woman's rights in every sphere of life. Helen Felmere's obstinacy in asserting these rights brings on all her difficulties, as will be shown in a later analysis on woman's rights in Chapter 5. With the writing of this first novel around such issues, Elliott would find her religious and political convictions leading her increasingly toward the battle for woman's rights.

Another important theme is articulated early in this first novel: the matter of "honor." Honor here is not simply personal integrity but a code of honor, typically Southern, which absorbed and fascinated Elliott so much that it became the subject of several short stories and was used again and again as the *modus operandi* of longer works.

Should Helen break her oath to the cousin-husband she does not love? What prevents her from seeking Felix and happiness? "Nothing, save your word," her father replies, but this giving of one's word is more binding than all the oaths men may swear, for, says Hector, to break one's word would be "breaking faith; and all the world holds this code of truth to your neighbor" as the ultimate law which prevents disorder and anarchy in society (58).

The code of honor is utterly binding. No mitigating circumstances can change a course of action once one has pledged his honor. Pursuing the implications of her decision to their bitter conclusion, the heroine must choose to give up her own child and finally her life. The dark hint of "fellness" in the surname *Felmere* which she bears, becomes fulfilled in her self-destruction. But honor is a two-edged sword. While on the one hand it protects society, on the other, if blindly held to for its own sake, it can produce an unyielding attitude of mind that admits of no arbitration or melioration, tragic and ultimately self-defeating.

The other side of honor, responsibility to self, is altruism, the giving of self to others. Without the ethical system of Christianity, what defense have the weak and the poor, asks Helen the rationalist. Why should anyone rationally contribute to the support of the nonproductive members of a society? Hector replies that one must support the poor and weak for the sake of future generations, for a time when education and natural selection will lift up virtue and goodness. If one cannot love one's fellow man as the Christian does, one must help him all the same, in order to preserve the well-being of the whole society. Is this "a passionless expediency?" she wants to know. Hector replies that it is "the glorious height of perfect philosophy" which will sustain and guide the noble spirit. Until education can raise all to an understanding of unselfish behavior for its own sake, Hector thinks Christianity with its rewards and punishments a useful way to keep the masses from transgressing (59–60).

In another lengthy dialogue on Reason and Religion, Felix Gordon is made the proponent of a forgiving, Christlike love. Helen counters with the Christian doctrine of eternal punishment for sinners, which she regards as inconsistent with the doctrine of love. Felix holds out for faith, but Helen sides with reason. Science will win out over Religion, she asserts.

These long arguments, so despised by the critics, show the author trying to find a basis for motivation. Lacking the framework of psychology, she must make her characters' personal creeds impel them to act. She is also trying to deal with one of the central concerns of the nineteenth century, the struggle with faith and doubt. It is no wonder the plot groans under the load of all this ratiocination. It is remarkable that characters so freighted with "ideas" should come off in any way resembling real human beings. Yet some do.

Individual portraits in the story, such as Mr. Tolman, a worldly priest, and Mrs. Vanzandt, a society matron, are deftly drawn from life. Lacking major roles, they are freed of the ideological machinery of the central characters and come off almost as well as some of Dickens's great minor portraits. Mr. Tolman, likened to Chadband by one character, is more interested in the Felmeres' marriageable niece than in saving the immortal souls of his parishioners. He is shown at his worst when he verbally duels with Helen about women who enter the religious orders. Helen defends the sincerity of such women as well as their good works, but the priest deprecates the sisterhoods, saying they are but "copying Rome" (180). Once asked, Helen breaks her self-imposed ban on expressing her opinions and roundly trounces Mr. Tolman with his own arguments. The society matron, Mrs. Vanzandt, befriends the lonely and rejected Helen, offers her a place to do her painting, and encourages her to assert her independence from what has become an intolerable marriage.

She shares Helen's independence of mind. Because of a similarly unhappy early marriage she has come to view the social skirmishes of upper class women as petty; she therefore chooses to live a rather eccentric life for one of her class; she does what she likes and meets only people who interest her. Mrs. Vanzandt is a maturely drawn and subtle character, skillfully used to tie various ends of the plot together. She is the New Woman Elliott liked so well to portray, of a type common in British and American fiction throughout the century from Hawthorne to Henry James.

The story conveys the impression of a deep pessimism in the mind of the author, and a spirit of uncertainty in the most fundamental tenets of her faith and her social and personal values. The story was written over the decade from 1869 to 1879, during the height of Radical Reconstruction in the South; it corresponded with the lowest ebb of the Elliott family's fortunes following their father's death. The depth of despondent questioning in the book transmits a sense of dislocation and even alienation underlying the outward banter and epistolary levity of the young author. Her first novel, like so many novels of the Southern Literary Renaissance half a century later, concerned itself with rapid change, violence, loss of faith and of identity, self-destruction, and death.

Critical comment about *The Felmeres* varied. The *Boston Globe* was totally unenthusiastic about Elliott's book and even misspelled the title, calling it an unfortunate "novel with a purpose. . . . As might be expected it is unnatural and possesses little interest as a work of fiction."[9] The *New Orleans Times* reviewer found it "more interesting than popular" because it had a religious theme; the *Boston Journal* found it hard to accept that a heroine should be an atheist. "Mr. Eliot" had written a powerful story nonetheless, "but it is most piteous and pathetic."[10] The *Pittsburgh Daily Telegraph* found it "a story of tender, dramatic power." The Philadelphia papers went both ways: the *North American* panned it; the *Inquirer* said politely that it was "admirably written"; the *Times* found it the "strongest and most promising book of the season."

The October 1879 issue of the *Literary News* indicated that Elliott's *The Felmeres* was tied for third place that season in the prize competition sponsored by the *News;* it ranked with a novel by Trollope and just after Tennyson's *Lover's Tale* in a list of fifty books published so far that year. Friends were soon writing that they had had difficulty finding copies. The book was still being read and quoted three years later: in June 1883 Robert Elliott wrote his sister

that a minister from Norwich, Connecticut, "one of our best men
. . . told me he had quoted *The Felmeres* in a sermon at the Pequot
House and wished to give [Sada] through me his very high appreciation of her work. . . ."[11] It was reissued in 1886 by Appleton, and a
new edition published by Holt appeared in 1895.

Later reviews continued to range from highly favorable to nega-
tive. Words most often used to characterize the story were "strange"
and "sad," "spirited and striking," or "startling finale." All reviewers
conceded skill in execution, but most were troubled by the fact that
the atheist heroine should be treated sympathetically and that her
trials should be so great and unremitting. Only a few caught the
point that Helen Felmere represented Rationalism personified. She
was the child of the new age of Facts, abandoned by her mother,
Orthodoxy, the American counterpart of the children of Dickens's
Gradgrind. Since the professed Christians in the book are depicted
as hypocritical and insincere, the virtuous atheist becomes the
means of casting scorn upon lukewarm Christians who fail to practice what they preach.

Margaret J. Preston, reviewer for the *Southern Churchman*,
compared *The Felmeres* with George Eliot's *Theophrastus Such:*
"Miss Elliott styles *The Felmeres* 'a novel'; and inasmuch as it has its
characters, its development of story, its dramatic situations, its vivid
realistic flow of talk, its unfoldings of individual qualities, it may
properly be called such; but it is a novel something in the line of
George Eliot's last—*Theophrastus Such*—a mere convenient vehicle through which to convey the author's idea of the restless,
questioning, unsatisfied and unhappy modern spirit of un-
faith. . . ."[12]

The reviewer for the *Nation* put his finger on the major problem
of the work: the avowed atheist is the stronger, more honest
character, while all the Christians are a bigoted, backbiting lot. The
atheist, with little to motivate her except honor and loyalty to her
dead father and his teachings, manages to live and die by her
convictions. Lack of firmer psychological motivation makes her
struggle seem unnecessary and her life one of bitterness and need-
less rejection.

Many readers were intrigued by the unusual theme. The reviewer for the *South Atlantic Monthly* of Baltimore went so far as to
pronounce it "powerful" and to liken the heroine to Antigone,
predicting that the author's "masculine strength and vigor of style,"

so remarkable for a woman writer, held for her a future of brilliant promise if she used her gifts wisely.[13]

Her brother Hab gave Sada Elliott a rather striking compliment by suggesting that only Hawthorne had gone before her in depicting such a heroine:

> In my humble opinion you have but one novelist this side of the Atlantic who will give you any trouble, and that is the author of the "Scarlet Letter," I believe Hawthorne. Had Helen once faltered the book would have been good but ordinary but she didn't falter, and it's a Waterloo and you are the Englishmen. It's a book with the greatest of questions to present and it does its work without shirking. Many a Tolman [the clergyman in the story] will swear at it clerically as they are called upon to answer, and most but not all will turn to it for their answer. A vast number of people will never understand it. . . . Talk as we may, we of the South are uneducated, ignorant, and rough [in the eyes of the North]. No novelist higher than a teller of tales—"Remus" has ever grown up in the land, barring yourself, and you have the right and honour of being the first.[14]

Habersham Elliott was correct. Though little fanfare heralded the fact, this was the first major novel by a Southerner to appear since the last Simms novel had been published in 1856. Twain, of course, was publishing, but no one thought of him as a Southern writer. Elliott's novel was followed a few months later by Cable's *The Grandissimes*, often given the honor of being the first Southern postwar novel. But Elliott had made the mistake of sticking to her religious and moral questions in this first novel and shunning the local-color elements a nation was eager to learn about. Thus *The Grandissimes* and its rivalry between the light and the dark brother is still read today, while *The Felmeres* has been so thoroughly forgotten that even library copies are extremely rare and hard to find.

IV *Frontier Tales*

The Texas territory was the setting for three short pieces, a character sketch and two lengthy short stories, the next of Elliott's apprenticeship work to appear in print. Unlike *The Felmeres*, which had had a strong resemblance to the mid-century British novel, these are very American in character and show Elliott turning toward the techniques of local color: regional dialects, frontier justice, much local scenery, and a strongly moralistic tone. Her plots were rather shaky in construction, as yet, and her scenery rather flat and two-dimensional, but despite their reliance on existing models by popular writers of the day, the works were good enough to be published in the periodical press, which afforded a ready market for almost any kind of local-color material.

The first published was "Jack Watson—A Character Study," which appeared in the *Current*, September 11, 1886. It is a dialect story of the Bret Harte sort—a tale of a local desperado named Jack Watson who has just been shot to death in San Antonio. The newspapers have written up his demise with a reformer's zeal, pronouncing judgment on him for his wicked deeds. The narrator, Jeff Sidberry, an old-time Texan, knew Jack Watson from the time he first came West, long before he became an outlaw. For the entertainment of his hearers bound for Corpus Christi on a long, hot train ride, Jeff unravels a tangled yarn about the early life of the notorious Jack.

Although basically a kind man at heart, Jack possessed a weakness for strong drink. When he drank, he would get careless with his six-shooters. Drinking one day while trying to clean his gun, he fired accidentally and fatally wounded his young wife, Letty. Too far from town for medical help, Jack kept a lonely death vigil in their cabin beside a water hole, fifteen miles from the nearest neighbor. In his grief at his wife's death, Jack became an outlaw, subsequently killing a sheriff. His friend still maintains that Jack had been a good man at heart, made violent by the hardships of frontier life, and that at the Last Judgment Jack Watson should be forgiven his sins. "The Lord air mussyful," Jeff concludes, "en air not no sheriff ner no Marshall" (167).

Despite the hard-to-read Kentucky-cum-Texas dialect of the narrator—which is interspersed with comments of the skeptical listeners—the author manages to convey sympathy for the grim existence of these frontiersmen. A tragic sense of life is communicated in what starts out as merely a colorful yarn.

A second literary gleaning from Elliott's 1885 Texas trip was a longer story entitled "A Simple Heart." It first appeared in the *Independent*, November 4, 1886, and was published as a book in 1887. Another frontier story, it concerns a carpenter who becomes a lay minister for the Episcopal Church in the out-of-the-way community of Pecan, Texas, one of those towns which boast a dozen bars but not a single church. Nat Carton and his schoolteacher wife work to build a place of worship for the townspeople. Nat's life as a simple carpenter is almost a parable; though barely literate, he is Christlike in his simple devotion to the church. Unfortunately, his rough-hewn ways of serving his fellow men go unappreciated. Once he has achieved his goal of constructing a church building, he is further humbled by his wife's dying of consumption.

The saloon keeper's wife, newly arrived from the East, convinces the growing town that it needs a real minister, one with the kind of social graces she had grown accustomed to back East. Sensing he is no longer wanted, the carpenter-priest hands over all his property to the diocese, including the church building, and disappears from the town of Pecan, headed for some other small town that can use his simple talents. As the years pass, the town's fleeting prosperity settles into a sleepy decline. Once again the people of Pecan remember their dedicated lay preacher and begin to understand what they have lost.

Elliott may have been familiar with Flaubert's famous story of the same name, "Un Coeur Simple," published in 1877. Learning of the frontier preacher, she may have called to mind the Flaubert story and the likeness between the simple, faithful old servant woman Félicité and her own main character, Nat Carton. Self-sacrifice is the theme in both stories.

There are many parallels between Elliott's story and the more famous Flaubert story. Both are told in the same style: they sweep over many years, use brief, clear sentences and short paragraphs, and concentrate on the movements, action, and dialogue of the central characters. The impact in both stories is created by depicting the hardships of a central character surrounded by unsympathetic minor ones. Neither story attempts to state a moral for the reader. Each character is shown to be endowed with a simplicity and directness that are partly inbred and partly environmental. Given only the most limited talents, each lives out a life of devoted self-sacrifice.

The basic plot of "A Simple Heart" must have been drawn directly from the experience of Bishop Robert Elliott. His sister, in fact, wrote him into the story as a young bishop making his first official visit to the town shortly before the old man decides to move away. And the author has given the story obvious parallels with the life of Christ. Nat Carton constructs a great wooden cross in front of his church, and this cross comes to symbolize the ingratitude heaped upon him by the townspeople. The story also sheds light on

the difficulty the bishop himself must have encountered in bringing
his ministry into meaningful contact with people of widely differing
backgrounds. What Elliott shows here is a *real* frontier where
ordinary people, not those of the sheriff-cowboy-Indian category,
live out their small triumphs and defeats. Elliott draws a parallel
between the harsh, dry land and the parched spiritual climate of
these men struggling to survive amid the lawlessness, materialism,
and hypocrisy of a frontier cattle town.

A third story dating from the Texas period, published soon after
"A Simple Heart," is a Texas tale of Romeo and Juliet with the
unlikely title "Mrs. Gollyhaw's Candy-stew."[15] It commences with a
social gathering at which the main entertainment is a taffy-pull, or
"candy-stew." The deceptively saccharin beginning soon gives way
to a deadly serious family feud which revives old Civil War hostilities and forgotten personal wrongs and ends with an unsolved
murder and the ironic accidental death of the murderer. The story
was reprinted in *An Incident and Other Happenings,* a collection of
Elliott's short stories published by Harper & Brothers in 1899.

Unfortunately, "Mrs. Gollyhaw's Candy-stew" displays a lack of
skill in storytelling largely overcome in later pieces. There are too
many characters, and they are indistinctly drawn. Embittered old
Mrs. Binkin seeks revenge for wrongs done her years before and at
the same time tries to protect her pretty young friend Milly
Conway, daughter of one of the feuding families, from suffering a
similar fate. A schoolteacher, introduced for romantic interest,
becomes embroiled in the feud, kills the murderer Billy Fleish in
self-defense, and is in turn blackmailed by Mrs. Binkin, who has
discovered his deed. The crosscurrents of allegiances among these
frontier families become further complicated by class and religious
differences, producing a plot that is out of focus and ultimately
weak.

The setting of the story is once again the town of Pecan, scene of
"A Simple Heart." The opening paragraph utilizes features of that
well-loved landscape, the bay and its savannahs, except that here
the bay is used metaphorically to describe the prairie as a sort of dry
sea:

. . . Across the vacant piece of prairie that crept like a bay into the town
of Pecan. For the prairie would assert itself, and wherever there was a
vacant place the cactus and mesquite and huisachie sprang up. Mrs.
Binkin's house fronted this great bay of prairie that a few hundred yards
away ended in an abrupt bluff; below this there was a river, and a stretch of

lowlands that spread as far as the eye could see; so that, looking from Mrs. Binkin's house, the gnarled live-oak-trees that edged the bluff were cut clear against the sky—a strange, weird outlook that very few, save Mrs. Binkin, cared for.[16]

The landscape is familiar, and so is the technique of starting with a flat picture in a frame and bringing it to life. Elliott had used the same technique in the opening paragraphs of *The Felmeres* and would do so again in *John Paget* (1893), a late novel. In the next few paragraphs the reader is presented with a view of the prairie in the springtime "framed in the wide-open back door," described like a landscape painting with foreground and background: "In the foreground a trim kitchen-garden, where in the borders a few roses bloomed royally; farther off, a strip of luxuriant clover with the cows knee-deep in it, and beyond, the prairie, that was now a great sweep of sunbathed blossoms—a limitless expanse all brown and orange and crimson with the velvety-soft coreopsis, and gleaming here and there the gold of the dwarf sunflower. A brilliant picture that redeemed the shabby hall, if Miss Anna-Bell had only known how to see it. . . ."[17]

After describing the interior of the house in relentless detail, the author finally sets the characters in motion and sends them moving out into this framed picture, which becomes "animated" by wind and sun and a single dark figure moving across it.

A flashback reveals the early wrong done Mrs. Binkin, her marriage out of spite, her life of bitterness, and the feud that these events provoked. The author then shows the reader the continuation of the feud as it revolves around the "Juliet" of this frontier romance, Milly Conway. Milly is being courted by Billy Fleish, a vengeful "Romeo" of the rival clan. Matters come to a head at the elaborate party put on by Mrs. Gollyhaw. Milly's brother is ambushed, shot, and tossed into a ravine by Billy Fleish. Billy is himself later killed by the schoolmaster Forbes, Milly's escort, on the way home from the party. Mrs. Binkin discovers Forbes's part in the night's mysteries and uses this knowledge to blackmail him into proposing to her friend Milly. Forbes finally makes a halfhearted proposal, is refused, and departs. Like one of the fates, Mrs. Binkin pursues the Fleish clan with reminders of their past wrongs and succeeds in driving them out of the district. Milly Conway eventually finds another suitor and Mrs. Binkin, satisfied, relishes her revenge.

In the midst of the violence and romantic turmoil of this complicated tale, Elliott was seeking ways of turning life into fiction with
techniques she had yet to master. Despite the weaknesses of
plotting a longer story, she displayed some ability at picturing the
life-styles of transplanted Southerners, driven out by the Civil War,
who migrated westward in search of free land. It is the perpetuation
of regional traits—the pretensions, provincialisms, and feuding
ways—that they carried west with them which Elliott tried to depict
in her elaborately contrived plot.

V   Americans Abroad

A second group of apprenticeship sketches and short stories,
produced during the 1880s, was based on Elliott's 1887 travels in
Europe and the Holy Land. They consisted first of sixteen sketches
written en route while traveling through France, Switzerland, Italy,
Egypt, and finally Jerusalem, returning through northern Italy to
London, Oxford, and Stratford-upon-Avon. Second, there came a
group of short stories published in the *Independent* (1887–1888)—
"Miss Eliza," "An Idle Man," "As a Little Child," "A Florentine
Idyl," and "Stephen's Margaret." In addition, there were two later
pieces—"A Study of Song in Florence" (1902) and "Hybrid Roses"
(1906)—which were most likely written at the same time or based on
notes kept during the journey. European scenes in the novel *The
Making of Jane* (1901) were also derived from this travel experience.

Like all local-color writing, the sketches and short stories are
drawn from life—no imagined vistas or stock emotions. In this
group, though aware of Twain's *Innocents Abroad* (1869), Elliott
strove for freshness and originality, avoiding literary models. She
even displays enough self-confidence as a writer to inject into her
sketches comparisons with familiar views and sounds of her native
South. The sketches are full of telling details, humorous and often
satiric in tone, selected for their effect in pointing up incongruities.
The stimulus of travel provided not only fresh material but also
many vivid details and a tone that is lively and entertaining.

Prompted to write the same kind of on-the-spot journalism Twain
had used in his tour letters to the *Alta Californian*, Elliott had
contracted for a similar series of travel letters to be sent home for
publication in the *Courier-Journal*, although she never collected
hers into book form. She adopts the same irreverent, bantering tone
about what she sees and spends a great deal of time contrasting her

preconceptions with the real thing. Her use of satire and her contrasts between illusion and reality lend a new depth not present in her Texas stories and sketch.

Bursts of enthusiasm and occasional awe are interspersed with barbed comments about bad-mannered tourists or inhospitable natives. Elliott was awed, for example, at meeting H. M. Stanley of Stanley and Livingstone fame, but later observed acidly that he had "an obstinate-looking head," phrenologically speaking.[18] There was also a particularly obdurate hostel keeper in the Alps whose menacing reception of the tired travelers earned her the epithet "Modoc Squaw."[19] Elliott also describes a vast array of interesting and colorful characters encountered along the route, such as the incomparable Ali Mohammad, Chief Dragoman of Suez, whose rakish combination of Arab and Western garb made him look like "a stately gentleman who had dressed in a hurry to go to a fire."[20]

She was to encounter also many an unpleasant and unmannerly tourist. At Port Said there were Americans "of the kind one reads about. Perfectly self-satisfied; perfectly self-centered, despising everything they did not know, and believing firmly in everything American," being unspeakably rude to the French-speaking ship's crew because of the impenetrable language barrier.[21] On the other hand, there was a gossipy Englishwoman nicknamed the Red Rover "because of her coloring and general everywherewardness," a lady exactly four feet square whose tongue "pivoted like the needle of a marine's compass."[22]

Imagery is more abundant in the travel sketches than in any of Elliott's previous work, and wit lends them spice and pungency. She allows herself all the picturesque language that she carefully avoids in her quiet, studied short stories. Some of the comparisons are far fetched but oddly apt. For example, the shrill whistle of a French passenger train calls to mind the high piping chorus of frogs at sunset in the low-country rice fields back home. In Italy she notes parallels between twelfth-century family vendettas and those notorious family blood feuds in her native South.

What was to have been one of the high points of the trip became instead its greatest disappointment. She describes Jerusalem as a bad dream, full of unholy pilgrims, crowds of the gullible, and shrines of uncertain authenticity. Only the Wailing Wall struck the skeptical Elliott as a truly ageless shrine, where the litany of woe murmured by the faceless, changing crowd speaks for all the world's suffering.[23]

In the short stories from this period published in the *Independent*, characters begin to speak and move for themselves rather than like puppets mouthing the author's favorite ideas. A considerable amount of control has been achieved, for the style is spare and "under-written," combining smoothly all the elements that produce an acceptable work of fiction.

The first of these stories about Americans abroad, "Miss Eliza" (*Independent*, March 1887), concerns a Southern woman, elderly and homesick, living in Paris as the companion of her niece, an art student. Miss Eliza feels her life has been wasted. Long ago she rejected her only suitor out of a sense of duty to her brother, who lost his wife and needed help in rearing his daughter. She has lived entirely for others, with no life of her own.

Just before Easter, as she worships at the Cathedral of Notre Dame, she hears a familiar voice and recognizes her cousin Reginald, the man she once refused to marry. Now he has lost all of his family except his youngest son. He is alone and needs her, and has come to Paris to beg Miss Eliza to marry him and return to her beloved South.

But happiness and a chance to return home continue to elude Miss Eliza. Before she can respond, Reginald's child darts in front of a horse carriage. She manages to rescue him but is fatally injured and dies as Easter dawns—a soul too self-sacrificing for this world.

The sentimental little tale was probably written expressly as an Easter story to illustrate the idea of Christian sacrifice. The characters in the story, these Americans, seem to drift, almost against their will, homesick and ill at ease in their foreign environment, dwelling on past memories and lost hopes. At least Miss Eliza gets her last wish—her burial will take place at home, not on foreign soil. More than anything else, the story reveals the author's state of mind as she traveled with her ailing brother through Europe.

The next short story based on the 1887 journey was "An Idle Man," the only one of this group to be reprinted. It appeared as a filler to make up a book-length volume along with the short novel *The Durket Sperret*, published by Henry Holt in 1898. The two works had in common the fact that both were about courtship, and both have an unusual and not necessarily happy ending. In fact, three of the four stories in this group have love and courtship as subjects, and in each case the main female character is intelligent, independent, and unwilling to be easily won or to settle for a conventional marriage.

"An Idle Man" opens as a steamer is departing from the Bay of Naples bound for Port Said, carrying among its passengers one Melhis, a well-to-do gentleman traveling alone. One day Melhis happens to notice a young woman passenger and remarks on her directness of gaze and her independent manner. The young woman, Miss Morden, is accompanied by her father, a semiinvalid. Melhis soon becomes better acquainted with them and reveals that he is on his way to visit a friend in Australia. Everything about Melhis characterizes him as an idle man, apparently both wealthy and bored. Assuming he has nothing better to do with his life, Miss Morden lectures him on his idleness.

By the time they reach Suez, the elder Morden's health has deteriorated. Since Melhis had once studied medicine, he offers to disembark and help Miss Morden care for her father. As the good samaritan cares for the invalid, he finds that he has fallen in love with the grave, intelligent young woman and asks her father if he may speak to her of marriage.

But before Melhis can propose, a rival appears on the scene, a man named Nevil whom Miss Morden has recently met and grown to like. Misinterpreting her friendship with Nevil as a romantic commitment, Melhis decides to continue his trip to Australia, leaving the matrimonial field to his younger competitor.

After Melhis's departure, Miss Morden learns from Nevil the true nature of her mysterious traveling companion. Far from being an idle man, Melhis is actually a philanthropist, a man of vast wealth who makes it a practice to be of assistance to others. "Noblest man I know," Nevil says of him.[24] Miss Morden has not only misjudged Melhis but, by her misguided attempts to reform him, has forfeited an exceptional matrimonial opportunity. The narrative device used here, and in several of the stories of this period, is similar to that in "Jack Watson," where layers of incorrect impressions are peeled away to arrive at the real personality beneath the facade.

"As a Little Child," the next short story, draws heavily upon Elliott's own disillusioning experiences in Jerusalem. The main character, a young preacher from Arkansas, finds that the religious pilgrimage has undermined rather than strengthened his faith.

In the story, Brother Hardin and a party of fellow pilgrims arrive in Jerusalem on a cold, rainy day at the crowded Easter season. Unable to find suitable hotel accommodations for his fiancée, Miss Mandy Pouder of Swampedge, he turns for assistance to another party of Americans staying at the hotel. The Arkansas fundamen-

talists are contrasted with this group of upper-class Easterns, Angli-
cans by persuasion, who do not take such a literal approach to their
faith and who view the religious landmarks and relics with a
degree of skepticism. Confronted with the doubtful authenticity of
the shrines, Preacher Hardin believes that everyone has lied to him.
His whole faith is shaken. "I've journeyed here for nothin'," concludes Preacher Hardin. "I've done lost all my religion sence I've
come here. . . ."[25] His fiancée meanwhile has absorbed these new
experiences with greater flexibility. Through the help of Emily, the
young Anglican tourist, she has come to a realization of the narrow-
ness of her own religious beliefs. She also begins to see her
preacher-suitor in a new light and knows that when she returns to
Arkansas she will not be able to bring herself to marry Mr. Hardin.

The third story, "A Florentine Idyl," contains some of the best
characterizations in any of these stories about Americans abroad. It
is further set off with touches of humor, as the female characters
reveal their small deceptions and narrow viewpoints to the reader
through their dialogue.

The story satirizes the social maneuverings of a group of middle-
aged American matrons who occupy a modest lodging house in
Florence, all of whom are trying to find wealthy husbands for their
eligible but impecunious daughters. They take an immediate dislike
to a young newcomer, a quiet, well-bred (and unmarried) young
woman who refuses to join in their games of gossip and social
pretense. Their matrimonial stratagems are unmasked when the
true identity of the young woman becomes known. With its satire on
American ex-patriates, the story has the flavor of one of Katherine
Mansfield's later stories, poking gentle fun at those who pretend to
be what they are not.[26]

"Stephen's Margaret," the last of the stories that Elliott sent to
the *Independent* (July 5, 1888), is a study of courtship among the
members of yet another colony of Americans making their home in
Italy.

Mrs. Vesey, a widow, spending a season in Rome with her
daughter Margaret and nephew Stephen Gwither, has taken rooms
at the Hotel du Sud because of its splendid view of the city. Their
stay is intended to afford Margaret the opportunity for broadening
her experience with the world before she settles down in marriage.
Until now it has been assumed that she will marry her cousin
Stephen. Soon, however, another young man, one Taunton,
presents himself as a candidate for Margaret's affections. Taunton,

who is a scholar of thirteenth-century antiquities, takes Margaret with him everywhere to instruct her in his favorite subject. Stephen, meanwhile, looks on, wondering if Margaret will ever return his years of devotion to her

Taunton's eventual proposal of marriage is couched in terms not of love but of intellectual companionship, offering Margaret the prospect of a life of looking after his needs while he carries on his studies. Love and mutual sharing are essential to a happy marriage, Margaret decides, and rejects Taunton's proposal. Having given Margaret an opportunity to mature and see the world, Stephen finds his gamble has paid off, for, despite their many disagreements, Margaret belongs to *him*. [27]

The story unfolds largely through dialogue, giving it a modern, sophisticated air, much superior in the telling to Elliott's first frontier pieces. The author stays in the wings, letting the characters reveal themselves through their words and actions.

Of the two later stories which use material from the European experience, the first, "A Study of Song in Florence," which appeared in the "American Girl Abroad" series in *Harper's Bazar,* is a rather conventional piece of freelance journalism about how to live cheaply abroad while getting the most for one's educational dollar. It is mentioned here only to demonstrate how thriftily Elliott retained every bit of material she had to work with until she could find the right setting for it.

The last story utilizing foreign travel material, "Hybrid Roses," appeared in *Harper's Monthly* in 1906. It returns to the problem of the American's search for identity, and it utilizes the device of illusion versus reality which runs through this entire group of stories. It explores a favorite Elliott theme—the role of heredity, of education and environment in the making of a gentleman, or in this case a gentle*woman.*

As the story opens, Elizabeth, only daughter of a wealthy American family, has begun to speculate on how her grandfather acquired his great wealth and why he built his "ancestral home" to look like an English country house, complete with extensive and well-landscaped grounds and huge rose garden. Not even her English nurse, who has been with Elizabeth all her life, will reveal much of her grandparents' history to her, though Nanny had apparently known the old folks before they came to America. Elizabeth suspects that Nanny may even be her own great-aunt. A trip to England gives Elizabeth a chance to trace her ancestry. Part of the mystery of her background is solved when, outside a small village, she comes upon an estate that is almost identical to her own "ancestral home." It is revealed that her grandparents had been in service here and that her grandfather was once the gardener for the estate. With his newfound wealth he had duplicated both the house and gardens in America.

Elizabeth comes back to America unsure of her status in society, shamed at the thought of having had working-class grandparents. She feels she can never attain any real social standing because her origins are humble and her wealth all "new" money. An odd impulse to make up for what she regards as the pretense of her forebears causes her to hire out as a housemaid so that she can study how the servant class lives. The experiment leads her to a new appreciation of hard work and ambition and the value of "getting ahead." She determines to reveal to her titled English fiancé that she is at best a "hybrid rose," like those in her own rose garden, transplanted from English soil. Her future husband reveals that he too is something of a hybrid, and that his title is based on achievement, not inherited wealth.

The question of what constituted true gentility was one often raised by Elliott, who placed higher value on upbringing, taste, and attitude than on wealth as a yardstick of social position. Upward mobility was acceptable and good, for it meant that parents were seeking a higher cultural standard for their children and that society would thus improve with each generation. Hybridizing on these terms is as good for people as for roses, Elliott seems to be saying. It is as though in this story Elliott's Americans abroad at last come to terms with themselves and their background.

Experimentation with frontier or European settings and with a variety of subjects, characters, and themes had taught Elliott the rudiments of her craft but had not produced what would come to be her most important contributions to the local-color phase of the Realistic Movement in American literature. Following the advice of Constance Fenimore Woolson, she began upon her return home in 1887 to depict, as in a vast diorama, the pre- and postwar South she knew best, for the national audience she had hoped to reach—the readers of *Harper's*, *Scribner's*, *Lippincott's*, and *McClure's* magazines.

CHAPTER 3

The Regional Experience

T HE American experience between the Civil War and the
First World War was characterized by change in every sphere
of life. In attempting to comprehend and express the many changes
around them, writers responded in several ways; the literature of
the period abounds with themes of conflict. One response was an
intense regionalism which sought to record the uniqueness of New
England or the expanding West or parts of the South even as a more
settled way of life was vanishing.

In *Harvest of Change* (1969) Jay Martin has documented the
restless preoccupations of an age which saw the rapid rise of wealth,
the growth of cities, social reform, the growing importance of
science and its quarrel with orthodox religion, and the advent of
new technologies, bringing within reach every kind of machine from
typewriters to locomotives.[1] The response of many Southern writers
to change and cultural dislocation, Martin points out, was a retreat
to the more secure and predictable past, creating a romantic and
nostalgic view of life before the Civil War that was part fact, part
myth. Thomas Nelson Page glorified "befo' de wah" plantation life
by putting into the mouth of the character Negro Sam in "Marse
Chan" (1884) such sentiments as these: "Dem wuz good old times.
. . . Dyar warn no trouble nor nuttin." Page's stories of old Oakland
plantation, with its cavalier gentlemen and ladies, its docile and
happy slaves, put him at the forefront of the local-color movement.
Local color, with its scene painting, regional dialects, and cataloging
of differences in attitude and ways of life, looked back upon a golden
age now lost.

Some regionalists, contrasting the troubled present with the
glowing past, developed a strong sense of the ironic. Looking at the
South, with its still unsolved Negro question, George Washington
Cable expressed this irony so forcefully in his later writing that he
was compelled to leave New Orleans for Massachusetts. For many

other writers romance gave way to realism. There were too many limitations in the earlier views of the old regime, Jay Hubbell points out in *Southern Life in Fiction* (1960). Increasingly, literary themes involved the postwar struggle for survival, adaptation to poverty and to a changing social order. However, there were risks: "If a novelist treated realistically the relations between the races he was likely, as George W. Cable discovered, to find himself denounced as a Southern Yankee."[2]

Sarah Elliott was among those who rejected the romantic strain of local-color writing in favor of the realistic. In a review of *The Southern Plantation* for the *Sewanee Review* in 1924, she concurred with the author, Francis P. Gaines, that these were gross exaggerations on the part of Southern writers trying to explain or excuse the South for its perpetuation of slavery, and that the writers of such old plantation myths were not, after all, "'to the plantation manor born,' in short were aliens, laying monstrous stress on the glory of the masters as opposed to the misery of the slaves" (335). Elliott felt compelled, as one who *had* been part of that life, to tell her version of it, and to set the record straight through the use of the newly emerging techniques of Realism. Unquestionably she stood with those writers who had given realistic descriptions of Southern life in the past, men such as A. B. Longstreet in *Georgia Scenes* (1835) and her own cousin William Elliott in *Carolina Sports* (1846).

Elliott returned from Europe and her meeting with Constance Fenimore Woolson determined to draw upon the Southern experience as she knew it, using Realism to counter these romantic myths, which she termed "Illusion on the Delectable Hill."[3] She saw, moreover, that the South shared the same problems, the same distressful dislocations in religion and morals, in politics and the changing social order, from which the rest of the nation suffered. She therefore did not confine herself to a single region or class, but sought for more universal themes and increasingly used the technique of indirection, allowing characters to reveal themselves to the reader.

By the 1880s the pages of such national monthlies as *Harper's*, *Scribner's*, *Lippincott's*, and the *Atlantic* bristled with local-color sketches and short stories, some of which were only atmospheric pieces or character sketches attempting to capture the distinctive qualities of a single region in terms of scenery and quaint "characters." A few writers, and Sarah Elliott was one of them, made an effort to search out universal themes and embody them in a good story.

So much local-color material from the South began to find its way into print that the literary field was soon crowded with writers hurrying to lay claim to this or that region: Cable had spoken for New Orleans; Mary Noailles Murfree had staked out East Tennessee; Woolson and De Forest had recently "done" Carolina. Elliott could well have settled for the tidewater rice and cotton lands of low-country South Carolina and Georgia as her literary province. But she chose not to concentrate on a single area, writing instead of many aspects of the South as she knew it, including a wide range of locales and social levels.

Her cast of characters was drawn at first from her own family and acquaintances—grandmother, brothers, cousins, maiden aunts—and their experiences. Gradually she widened the circle to include along with the impoverished gentry many black characters, the Tennessee mountaineers, the rednecks, professional men, merchants, veterans, and young women trying for the first time to make decisions and achieve financial independence.

The area around Beaufort, South Carolina (Kingshaven or Deep Haven in her fiction), was the heartland of her imagination; its stately homes, sheltering live oaks, and broad vistas over marsh and bay appear time after time in her work. Eventually, however, she moves away from the tidewater to other settings: the up-country towns, mountain coves, and sandhill villages about to become cities overnight with the coming of the railway. Plots which at first looked back on prewar life or the problems of postwar survival soon expand to include scenes of reconciliation between former enemies and—what was more difficult for some—adjustments to a rule of laws instead of frontier-style justice. Changing attitudes toward class and status, role conflicts, problems or finding "suitable" work for former aristocrats, and adjustments to the new technology abound in her regional stories and novels.

Her work throughout reflects her own point of view and her own aristocratic prejudices. Pessimistic at first, often ironic, her tone gradually becomes more optimistic, tolerant, and occasionally even humorous. A strong belief in free will, personal freedom, and pride in her region predominates. Like other regionalists, her tone becomes elegiac when she is describing an oligarchy which enjoyed both leisure and cultivation, whose wealth and hospitable largess seemed almost legendary, and whose way of life was so suddenly and irrevocably destroyed. For the most part, however, she makes a conscious effort to stand apart from this past, to depict society as a whole, "warts and all," to make a realistic minority report that is neither sentiment nor excuse on the region she knew best and the times through which she had lived.

Though published at different times throughout Elliott's career, the stories, novels, and other writings discussed here fall into a single series which, when arranged by internal chronology, reflects a regional response to the national problems of change. Here may be found not only some of her best work, but also some of the weakest. Four or five of her best stories, along with some weaker "fillers," were reprinted by Harper & Brothers in 1899 as *An Incident and Other Happenings*. B. Lawton Wiggins, who reviewed it for the *Sewanee Review* in April 1899, thought that it might well be "the best volume of short stories that has come to our notice this season," and that it had "more universal appeal than any book she had written" (246). The subject of Elliott's one late venture in biography was Sam Houston, a fellow Tennessean, who spent most of his life on the Texas frontier. Elliott singles out his struggles as a Southerner to keep Texas in the Union after sponsoring its hardwon statehood as the most crucial phase of his career.

The Durket Sperret is one of Elliott's most readable local-color novels because it tries to lift the Tennessee mountaineer out of the realm of stereotype and because it introduces Hannah Warren, the central character, as an independent "new woman" with aspirations for a better life. *John Paget*, on the other hand, tries (but fails) to examine in depth some of the attitudes of North and South toward such problems as the decline of orthodoxy, the growth of wealth, and the human problems that accompanied industrialization.

Many of Elliott's stories are full of pathos, a concession in part to the tastes of the growing number of women readers who preferred their stories that way. An overabundance of sentiment may also be attributed to Elliott's inability to maintain artistic detachment from material that was drawn so directly from personal experience. As social history, however, the regional stories are, for the most part, factual and restrained and contain much good development of character and accurate reportage. Looking back upon this regional literature in light of the Southern literary renascence of the twentieth century many observers would agree that Elliott's realistic, ironic vision is nearer perhaps than that of her romantic mythmaking contemporaries to what is seen today as the mainstream of Southern literature.

I   *"The Slate is Clean . . ."*

"Beside Still Waters," *Youth's Companion,* August 9, 1900, looks back to a generation before the Civil War to explain what plantation life was like in tidewater Kingshaven. As the story opens, Mrs. Bullen, the matriarch of the family, awaits word that her son has safely returned from a boat trip. The plantation boats were manned by oarsmen and were no match for the newfangled steamboats lately plying the coastal waters. To while away the anxious hours until her son's return, she delivers religious instruction to the house servants while her daughter Sophia reads from the Psalms. Neither technological nor social change was welcome, it would seem, beside the still waters of Kingshaven.

Mrs. Bullen muses on the question of education and moral instruction for the slaves, pointing out to her daughter that such a policy toward them had produced men like Anthony, an intelligent and trustworthy individual who kept accounts for the plantation and had been given authority over the other slaves as driver instead of a white overseer. He is undoubtedly the same Anthony referred to by Habersham Elliott as having been manumitted by his grandfather's will because of his years of service. Thus Elliott makes the story the occasion for restating the often-repeated argument that slavery had been justified because of the opportunity it afforded to educate and Christianize the African.

A similar statement about the relationship of the races before the Civil War appears in three stories about Miss Maria, a lovable but somewhat eccentric old lady of Kingshaven who lives alone, tended by the slave woman Kizzy and a coachman and man-of-all-work named Jack. In "Miss Maria's Revival" the question of religion is touched upon. Miss Maria has been swept up in a religious revival conducted by a Baptist preacher recently come to town. The normally staid and proper Episcopalian responds with unaccustomed enthusiasm to the preacher's exhortations, much to the consternation of Kizzy, who has never seen her mistress behave this way. Miss Maria finally decides to make a very large donation, much more than she can afford, to the cause of missions because of her enjoyment at being so stirred up.[4]

The second "Miss Maria" story, "Baldy," shows her involved in a dispute with her coachman over Miss Maria's aging coach horse, Baldy. The coachman wins and Baldy is put out to pasture in this somewhat patronizing little vignette.

The best of the three stories is "Faith and Faithfulness," designed to illustrate the kindly relationship between Miss Maria and Kizzy, presumably an effect of the moral instruction Kizzy has received. When the wartime occupation of her home town causes Miss Maria to become a war refugee, she flees to a mountain summer home with Kizzy and her family and is stranded there for some months without money. The other servants, hearing of free land to be distributed by the new government, go home to claim their share, leaving Kizzy to provide somehow for herself, her own small children, and Miss Maria. Kizzy hires out by the day for wages, working for a Northern clergyman's family while Miss Maria stays home to look after Kizzy's children.

Kizzy's employer soon learns of Miss Maria's plight and Kizzy's faithfulness. He sends them food and firewood, but only succeeds in wounding the old lady's pride. At this, Kizzy, who identifies completely with her mistress's attitudes, announces that she is going to quit her job. The clergyman and his wife pay a call upon the household and are surprised to be received in Miss Maria's shabby parlor lighted with candles in ornate silver candlesticks—the last remnants of Miss Maria's former wealth. Proudly she presents a pair of candlesticks to the astonished couple, explaining that of course she cannot accept charity. The otherwise sentimental tale is redeemed by its gently humorous tone and its unusual treatment of the difference in attitude between the proud Southerner and her Yankee benefactor, as well as the reversal of roles of mistress and servant.

A longer and better-written story called "Some Data" explores several of these subjects in greater depth. The four-part story appeared in a collection edited by Mrs. K. P. Minor of Richmond called *From Dixie* (1893), a commemorative volume designed to raise funds for a Confederate memorial. Other stories and poems in the volume were contributed by well-known Southern authors: Sidney Lanier contributed "To Lucie"; John Bannister Tabb, "Indians" and "Solitude"; and there were stories by James Lane Allen and Thomas Nelson Page.

Like so many of the stories by Elliott which span the war years, "Some Data" is drawn from life. The hero is the barely fictionalized portrait of Sarah Elliott's cousin, General Stephen Elliott, a native of Beaufort (who because of a similarity of names was often mistaken for Bishop Elliott's son). The general had taken part in the second defense of Fort Sumter and was later wounded in the Battle of the Crater at Petersburg, Virginia, in July 1864. He returned to Beaufort but found his home occupied by a federal general and was obliged to live in an overseer's cabin on his former plantation, helped by his own former slaves, now freedmen. Unable to regain title to his land, he caught and sold fish for a living. The aftereffects of his wounds brought about his death in 1866.

This well-known story of the doomed aristocrat was not easy to cast as fiction. To give it a "frame" Elliott adds a narrator in the person of Robin, a clergyman, who has grown up with the dashing and impetuous former planter named Ted. The story is structured around a series of contrasting scenes before, during, and after the war. A sportsman and playboy in his youth, Ted goes to war and becomes a hero. But upon his return he finds that his lands and livelihood are gone and he has no way to survive. The clergyman cousin, on the other hand, has prepared for one of the professions and has his salary to sustain him in the period of general economic collapse.

In the first episode, Ted is shown as a not-too-serious college student, home on holiday, who spends his time at sports and takes part in a devil-fishing expedition, such as the one described by William Elliott in *Carolina Sports*, where a giant manta ray is harpooned and allowed to tow a small boat for miles in the manner of a Nantucket whaler. In the next episode, Ted wins the heart of Isabel, Robin's childhood sweetheart, and marries her himself. An apparent winner in every sphere of life, Ted epitomizes the romantic view of the planter so often drawn in Southern fiction. But in Elliott's story there is a dramatic reversal which begins even as Ted is shown in the third episode heroically defending "a pile of bricks"—all that is left of Fort Sumter by this stage of the war.

Seriously wounded, Ted returns to find his home occupied by federal troops. He has nowhere to house his wife and sons until he is offered the overseer's cabin on what had formerly been his own plantation. A former slave befriends him, accompanies him on fishing trips, and helps him sell the fish door to door.

Overcome by hardship, unable to adjust to life under the new conditions, Ted is dying of his wounds, comforted in the last scene by his wife and his cousin Robin. Wandering in a delirious dream of the past, he interprets the flowers brought to him by Robin as a peace offering from his former enemies and dies reconciled. The jonquils he has requested come from the garden of the plantation house, planted there by his mother years before. Robin has picked them but, in an uncharacteristic moment of rage and frustration, he has pulled up all the bulbs and destroyed them, symbolizing a way of life that has vanished and will never "flower" again.

Once again, Elliott's story is spare and well constructed, developing a familiar subject in a somewhat different way by use of a narrator and through contrasting scenes; the sports fishing expedition and the selling of fish for a living, the downfall of the cavalier planter, and the survival of the modest professional man.

In the story's concluding paragraphs, Elliott writes her final word on the vanquished South, a kind of confession and absolution for the sins of the past: "It is not often given to a people to suffer as the Southern people have suffered, and whether the war was their own fault or whether it was a judgment on them for their sins of omission and commission, or 'negligence and ignorance,' is between them and their God. But whatever was the account against them, it has been wiped out, with a sponge dipped in tears and blood, and the slate is clean for the score of this new generation—this 'New South.' God help them."[5] And the story ends with words of forgiveness uttered by the dying man: "It has been a hard fight to forgive my enemies, Robin, but I've won; and for reward the stranger people have sent me all the jonquils."[6]

Twice more in later stories Elliott used flowers as symbols of continuity of tradition and a link with the past. She was fond of flowers and was an enthusiastic gardener; thus the symbols came naturally to her. In "Miss Ann's Victory" Easter lilies in bloom become the means of revelation at the climax of the story,[7] and in another, "Hybrid Roses," the flowers in the title symbolize the new Americans, transplanted from their native Europe, who are hardier and more adaptable than the parent stock from which they sprang.[8]

For its view of prewar Carolina plantation life and the effect of the war's aftermath upon individuals, "Some Data" has special interest, since in this story Elliott tried to link the era of William Elliott's *Carolina Sports* with that of the Reconstruction. The closing section, dealing with the Charleston people's strong enmity for their "conquerer," may be compared to De Forest's *The Bloody Chasm* (1881). Constance Fenimore Woolson has dealt with the same bitter feelings in the short story "Rodman the Keeper" (1880). In these two stories by non-Southerners, the unforgiving pride of the South is the motivating force. The native writer, on the other hand, in dealing with the same subject of wounded Southern pride, ends her story with words of forgiveness and reconciliation.

The same reconciliation theme occurs in three later stories Elliott published over a period of twenty years. All are set in that part of the Deep South which suffered the most devastation, the area affected by two years of occupation and the "scorched earth" of Sherman's march. In them there are reunions with former enemies. A prodigal son returns, a friendship is restored, a new understanding is gained or a moral victory won. The author is dealing in every case with intense emotions and painful memories, and one can sense behind the spare and careful wording much bitterness and regret; yet even the bleakest of these stories is occasionally relieved by some flash of humor. They are stories from a time when literary taste permitted, even encouraged, the display of pity, terror, and remorse.

The first of Elliott's stories in the order of events of the postwar period being treated is "Jim's Victory" (*Book News*, October 1897), which concerns the desperation of a refugee planter family in the first days and weeks following the cessation of hostilities, and the compromises of their pride necessary for their survival. Once again we find a story that is full of autobiographical detail. Two brothers have returned home from the fighting: Jim, an officer, and Tom, a schoolboy who had run away to enlist in the last months of the war. Jim has been allowed to bring his horse home with him, but he must sign a loyalty oath to the federal government to be allowed to keep it. He has been unable to bring himself to sign. Tom turns peddler and tries to barter household goods and homemade millinery in return for badly needed food. He goes off for a week to peddle his wares at nearby farms, but he is intercepted by federal officers who try to confiscate the horse. He feigns mental illness and manages to escape, but on the way home he comes down with an attack of malarial chills and fever. The courageous example of his young brother Tom makes Jim reconsider; he swallows his scruples and takes the oath, so that the family can keep the horse and thereby have a better chance to survive.

Though filled with pathos and melodrama like all the narratives in this group, the story is otherwise well told and the characters are convincing. The incidents, typical of many such dilemmas faced by wartime survivors, give the story suspense, a dramatic climax, and a satisfying outcome.

"After Long Years" (*Youth's Companion*, April 23, 1903) reunites two acquaintances, once wartime enemies, who had aided one another after being wounded in battle. A generation later, the son of the Yankee soldier discovers his father's Southern friend ill and living in poverty. He helps to bring about a mutually favorable lease of the Southerner's land and a meeting between the two veterans. The reconciliation theme here is somewhat marred by the unlikely coincidences involved.

"Some Remnants" (*Youth's Companion*, April 18, 1901) also works toward an attitude of understanding and reconciliation, but its material, Gothic and grotesque, makes it less successful. A surveyor laying out the right-of-way for a new road stumbles upon a large, dilapidated house and watches awestruck as a strange charade is enacted. An aging war veteran marches out of the house, drills a company of imaginary troops, receives a flag from one of two elderly women standing on the front porch, then marches silently away. The surveyor sees this scene reenacted twice more on successive days. The bewildered onlooker finally learns from a local resident that the veteran had returned home injured and bereft of his reason, and that the townspeople have helped to support him and his sisters ever since. Everyone understands his compulsion to reenact this one triumphant ceremony from his past. Now that the road is going to cut across the man's property, they fear that some unsympathetic witness might laugh or cause the sick man to become violent. The surveyor arranges for the road to bypass the house so that the privacy of the three old people will be maintained. Bizarre as the circumstances may be, the story tries to make a statement about human concern and responsibility.

It is unfortunate that none of the stories described here has been reprinted in any collection of Elliott's writings, for they are only to be found today in the often-unindexed files of the magazines in which they originally appeared. Their point of view and accuracy of detail make them at least of interest as historical footnotes to that dark period, even though they cannot qualify as great literature.

II *Southern Justice*

The next group of stories in the order of events of the war and its aftermath describes the Southerners' problems in adjusting to a system of government by laws, not men—problems in permitting courts to settle disputes rather than taking the law into their own hands.

Three of these stories are among Elliott's best: "An Incident," "Without the Courts," and "Squire Kayley's Conclusions." The first two appeared originally in *Harper's* in 1898 and 1899, and the third in *Scribner's* in 1897. All were reprinted by Harper & Brothers in the collection *An Incident and Other Happenings* (1899). A facsimile reprint of *An Incident* was reissued by Books for Libraries Press, Short Story Index Reprint Series, in 1969, making it the only Elliott book now in print.

The title story, "An Incident," concerns the threat of sexual assault of a white woman by a Negro servant, an extremely inflammatory subject at the time it was published because threats to "Southern womanhood" could still call out night-riding lynch mobs in the deep South. Elliott was to write other stories on similarly controversial or emotional subjects, but most of them never found their way into print, as we shall see in discussing problems of the New South.

Miss Nellie, wife of a Southern farmer, Joe Morris, is threatened by an ax-wielding servant, Abram. Frightened, she pushes off in a small boat tied nearby and escapes her attacker. When Morris returns home from a trip and cannot locate his wife, the other servants describe what happened. Not waiting to find his wife, Morris gathers his neighbors to form a posse. Meantime the Negro Abram has been captured and is being held in jail.

The boat carrying Miss Nellie has drifted down river and is finally spotted by fishermen. They rescue her and put her on the train for home. Although she informs her husband that she is safe and has not been harmed, the posse is determined to break into the jail and lynch the servant Abram anyway. The sheriff, in order to protect the prisoner until he can receive a fair trial, knows that he will have to fire upon his friends and neighbors who make up the posse. Secretly he arranges for Abram to be smuggled away in a wagon while he stands off the mob. Before a pitched battle can take place, the circuit court judge arrives and calls off the mob just as they discover the prisoner has been removed.

The black man is speedily sentenced and imprisoned. Years later a white teacher who regularly visits the prison meets Abram and learns his story. Although bitter at the harshness of his sentence, Abram is reconciled to life imprisonment. Jim Crow laws and other forms of intimidation of black people have made life little better than a prison term anywhere in the South. In the last paragraph the teacher then muses upon what will eventually solve the Negro problem. Elliott does not take the opportunity to deal with the white South's failure to offer the Negro opportunities for education; she merely leaves the paragraph as a kind of wishful afterthought.

A reviewer for the *Nation* recognized the story as an uncommon one for its time and place: "Apart from questions of artistic value, the world is interested in a Southern woman's presentation of the lynching problem. But it is not the least proof of the author's skill that she relies so slightly on the adventitious; that, in reading, one is able to forget, until recalled by the feebleness of the last paragraph, that the problem is of the present. In its severity of outline, swift movement, sinister suggestion of more than meets the eye, the sketch shows qualities which should make for its endurance."[9]

"An Incident" may have been based on actual events which took place in South Carolina. In 1893 a Negro suspected of rape, John Peterson, was transferred without adequate guard from a place of detention back to the town where the crime occurred, and was lynched. Writing about this celebrated case, N. G. Gonzales, editor of the crusading *State* newspaper, took a strongly antilynch stand and wrote a headline proclaiming the innocence of the accused. There had been reasonable doubt as to the man's guilt, but the governor, Ben Tillman, had failed to provide proper guards. Feeling ran so high over the issue and Gonzales's censure of the governor and the mob that he was burned in effigy in the town of Barnwell. And on another occasion, just a year before Elliott published "An Incident," Gonzales had said in an editorial defending a man lynched by a mob for barn burning: "Property, then, in the enlightened judgment of these barbarians, is more sacred than life. . . . How can lawlessness rebuke lawlessness, or crime discourage crime?"[10]

Hyder Rollins points out that Elliott's characterization of Abram in "An Incident" is perhaps the first instance where the "brute Negro" is depicted as lawbreaker in fiction by a Southerner.[11] But, having thus shown the lawless side of the man's character, she must have felt constrained to mitigate the picture somewhat. In her last paragraph she implies pessimistically that the society which had withheld an education from Abram had contributed to the problem, and that its resolution would not soon be forthcoming. Wade Hall has also remarked on the portrayal of the Negro in this story (while incorrectly titling it "An Accident").[12]

In the light of such inhumanity and injustice, one may well ask why Sarah Barnwell Elliott did not speak out more militantly in behalf of Negro rights, Negro suffrage, and education for the Negro, as she was to do for the woman's rights cause. Neither her upbringing, the temper of the times, nor the unfortunate example of braver writers like Gonzales and George Washington Cable encouraged her to be more courageously outspoken.

When Cable had published "The Freedman's Case in Equity" (1885) and *The Negro Question* (1888), he had encountered such a storm of protest in the national and local press that he finally moved, as had been said, from New Orleans to New England, so vitriolic and hostile was the criticism.[13] Cable was prompted by strong and sincere religious convictions to speak out in behalf of the Negro's civil rights, on prison reform, and on the evils of the convict-lease system. In a temperate and balanced appraisal of deteriorating opportunities for the black man in the South during the 1880s, Cable advocated education and more informed use of the ballot box as the greatest hope for alleviating the problem. The right to vote had gradually been denied the Negro population through a combination of "grandfather clauses," poll tax maneuvers, and acts of intimidation. Cable perceived that the Negro was not alone in his plight, for the poor white in many areas was caught in the same predicament.[14]

Strong religious conviction had motivated Cable, as it also had Elliott. But her own background and the relative immobility of women in the Southern caste system prevented her from making a more forthright attack on this aspect of Southern mores. By adding a paragraph to the story of Abram in which she echoed Cable's ideas about education, she had gone as far as any moderate dared who hoped to continue living in the South.

Another study of Southern justice, "Squire Kayley's Conclusions," the "happening" in *An Incident and Other Happenings*, is one of Elliott's best stories—both realistic and ironically humorous. The setting is the town of Greenville in the South Carolina piedmont, at some time in the 1880s. Squire Kayley, a local attorney, is determined to teach his potential clients to utilize the courts as a means of settling their disputes. He finally persuades one Negro client to bring suit to obtain legal redress and wins the assault and battery case in his behalf. Later the squire agrees to represent a white man, Nick Tobin, in an alienation-of-affection suit against Loftus Beesley, who has run off with Nick's wife. By the suit the squire hopes to prevent a duel, which any question of a man's honor requires. But the squire finds that public opinion is now turning against the aggrieved husband in favor of the guilty wife, since the husband has not exercised his time-honored right to gun down his rival. The townspeople say that Squire Kayley is immoral in trying to reduce all the town's transgressions to a question of suing for damages in a court of law. Nick Tobin presses and wins his case and is paid damages, but the townspeople criticize him severely for spending money he has apparently won by his wife's ruin. Squire Kayley realizes the town has much yet to learn about modern justice!

This same matter of the need for settlement of grievances within the law is nowhere more powerfully stated than in the third of these stories, "Without the Courts" (also included in *An Incident and Other Happenings*), perhaps the most grimly realistic of all Elliott's stories. The particulars of a duel are gradually revealed through gripping suspense, and the surprise ending is thoroughly convincing. George Beverley has sent for his lawyer, a relative called Tad, to arrange for the sale of his homeplace and the distribution of his property to support his wife and child, whom he suddenly announces he is sending to Europe. This unexpected news on a quiet morning in the low country brings forth strong protest from his attorney. How can Beverley sell the home which has meant so much to generations of his family? Beverley is adamant. A group of buyers will purchase the house and land for a hunting club, the name will be changed, and the place will be gone out of the family and forgotten. "Traditions? Memories? All marred and blotted— *stained*," the troubled man adds incomprehensibly.[15] Lise Beverley, his wife, suddenly arrives home, trembling with shock, to announce that her cousin Sandy Bowman has been shot—found dead after an early-morning hunting trip. All hurry to "The Point," a neighboring plantation, where the Bowman cousins live. Throughout a long and disturbing day, hints gradually reveal that the dead man was suspected by Beverley of being his wife's lover. In challenging his rival to a duel, Beverley chose to use a shotgun so that if either was killed everyone would assume that there had been a hunting accident.

"Squire Kayley's Conclusions" and "An Ex-brigadier," "Without the Courts," and the title story of *An Incident and Other Happenings* are by far the best of the Harper collection. They did much to strengthen Elliott's growing reputation as a realistic writer. The *Nation* reviewer commented on her choice of subject: "These studies, for the most part of Southern types far removed from the mountaineer and negro who have more than borne their part in fiction, point hopefully to a larger work in this direction. Southern writers have appeared to stand in need of the Gilbertian injunction, 'Spurn not the nobly born,' so careful has been their avoidance of the higher social orders. Miss Elliott's observations show the sympathy of one who is part of what she describes, yet they are as evidently made with clear eyes not sealed by tradition. The field before her is a rich one."[16]

III   *Covites of the Cumberland*

The white planter class and the black people of the Deep South were not Elliott's only subjects for local-color fiction. Having lived for twenty years or more in the mountains of Tennessee in close touch with the rugged backwoodsmen, she devoted an entire novel to the inhabitants of the mountain valleys of the Cumberland, with whom she frequently traded and in whose school she sometimes taught.

The Cumberland Mountains harbored a quaint, proud, and stubborn group of people, descended from Scotch-Irish settlers, who had followed the watercourses until they found hills that resembled their homeland. The "covites" of the Cumberland valleys or coves had unusual speech patterns and rigid social customs which made them ideal raw material for the pen of the regional writer.

Since Mary Noailles Murfree had already taken the hill folk of East Tennessee as her special subjects for study, Elliott stayed away from them until in *Jerry* (1891) she finally selected a backwoods character for her hero. But she felt that one could still do something original with a subject if it were handled deftly, and she continued to write about the social distinctions and levels within the covite society and the impact of change upon the older generation. Elliott shows an insider's knowledge of their manner of living which is lacking in Miss Murfree's accounts because the latter knew her mountaineers mainly through summer visits to the mountains of Tennessee rather than from continuous experience.

Elliott had prepared a sketch she originally called "The Covites of

the Cumberland Mountains" and offered it to Edward Bok, editor of
the *Ladies' Home Journal*, in the spring of 1896. It was one of the
first pieces she was able to sell after settling in New York. The title
of the piece finally became "A Race That Lives in Mountain Coves"
and the article was run at last in the issue of September 1898, more
than a year and a half after Elliott had been paid for it. It proved to
be a fairly conventional and somewhat patronizing feature story with
much dialogue that revealed the covites' character—shrewd, stoic,
shy, and proud. The curious conversational circumlocutions of the
group are used extensively.

Elliott's description of the Cumberland plateau in the article
demonstrates her complete familiarity with the region and even
suggests perhaps a touch of homesickness as well:

The scenery is not wild, but it is very beautiful; the mountains are clothed
from base to apex with a heavy forest growth of great variety, showing
numberless shades of exquisite green in the spring, and in the autumn
breaking into waves of scarlet and purple and gold that seem to burn like
fire through the haze of Indian summer. In winter a fall of snow covers all;
great icicles hang from cliffs, and the bare trees bend and sway beneath the
burden of the frost fringe that yet looks so fairylike. The first warm wind in
February sweeps it all away into the roaring, rushing streams that foam
about the great rocks, or burrow under them, and at last with a cry dash
over the cliffs and away to the valleys below.[17]

Preparation of the magazine article in turn suggested to Elliott
the possibilities of a longer story, which she swiftly completed and
published, a novel originally called "As Others See Us" but later
entitled *The Durket Sperret*. It ran serially in *Scribner's* from
September to November 1897 and was published by Henry Holt
and Company in 1898.

The "sperret" of the title refers to the pride and stubbornness of a
class-conscious cove family, the Durkets. Grandmother Warren, a
Durket before marriage, has so much of this "sperret" that she is
likely to "pitch a fit" of pure anger when crossed.

Orphaned Hannah Warren, heroine of the novel, lives in Lost
Cove, a mountain valley near Sewanee, Tennessee, with her Warren grandparents. The old people had been comparatively well off
until their sons left home and the eldest, Hannah's father, was killed
felling a tree; now they cannot carry on the farming alone. To
augment their meager income Hannah begins peddling vegetables

and dairy goods in Sewanee among the "Varsity people" who live on top of the mountain plateau.

Grandma pitches one of her famous fits when she learns that Hannah won't consent to marry her cousin Si Durket. Si is a drunken bully whom Hannah regards as a poor marital prospect even if he *is* a Durket. On his part, Si resents the fact that Hannah has stooped to peddling. Hannah herself, with much natural grace and good sense, does not find it demeaning. When Grandma's scolding becomes unbearable, Hannah takes summer work as a maid in one of the Sewanee households.

Hannah has her own share of the Durket "sperret" and is determined to resist efforts to "marry her off." When one of the university students, a young man named Dudley, notices Hannah and is nice to her, Si Durket grows jealous and spreads unfounded rumors about her virtue. To save her from embarrassment the university student offers to marry her, but she proudly refuses. Her decision gives the final blow to her grandmother, who pitches her third and, as it proves, fatal fit. The demise of the domineering old woman will make Hannah's lot easier to bear. The story ends abruptly here, as Hannah receives a marriage offer from Dock Wilson, a neighbor who has been running the farm in Hannah's absence. The university student learns he has also been jilted by Agnes Welling, Hannah's former employer, when she hears of his offer to Hannah. There is no happy ending with lovers united, but one gathers that, like other young women who are beginning to crave a measure of independence, Hannah will be able to manage her own life successfully.

One of the most interesting episodes occurs midway in the story when Old Dave Durket, Hannah's uncle, calls all his relatives to his deathbed. Elliott used the funeral customs among the covites to create a deathbed scene that would have done credit to Ambrose Bierce. Grandma Tildy Warren makes one of her rare journeys outside Lost Cove to be present at her brother's funeral and will-reading, hoping to receive her half of the family property, which her brother had taken away from her. A long-standing feud erupts between the dying man's two sons, Si and Dave, Jr. Si has often been cruel to his father and, in spite of the fact that he is the first son, he receives in the will only half his father's property. The weak-witted younger son's scheming wife proposes the brothers draw straws over the halves of the land. The younger brother draws the better half, including the house and barn, while Si draws the

pasture and family burying ground. The death scene, funeral, and
final disposition of the Durket property reveal through black com-
edy the true nature of the Durket sperret. It is an obstinate and
crippling rigidity, pride turned back upon itself. The chapter ends
with word from Si Durket that he intends to "plow up the buryin'
ground" and build his new house on it out of spite.

Several social strata in this mountain community are examined.
Certainly in Elliott's version not all mountaineers are lazy
moonshiners: most are hardworking freehold farmers proud of their
economic self-sufficiency and unwilling to be looked down upon by
anyone, least of all the "Varsity people"—who do nothing but "walk
about with books in their hands," according to cove people. The
archaic speech of the Cumberlands is faithfully reproduced, with
hain't and *air* for *ain't* and *are*, along with curious neologisms like
needcessity. The only false note is Elliott's use of "piazza"—a term
in the tidewater South for the wide verandah fronting larger
houses—in referring to the mountain cabin porch.

Hannah Warren is shown to be one of the new women of the age
of woman's rights, with ideas of her own and the will to work out her
own destiny rather than to submit to what she knows will be an
unhappy marriage. The given name "Hannah" was one Elliott had
always liked and had suggested to her brother Hab as a name for his
daughter. Like her fictional namesake, Hannah Elliott too became a
"new woman," a professional artist with studios at various times in
Paris and Rome.

The parallel societies of the covites and the university community
make for interesting dramatic contrast. Agnes Welling, a professor's
daughter at Sewanee—Hannah's employer and plot counterpart—
makes *her* own marital choice as firmly and independently as does
Hannah, the covite. The "civilizing" of Hannah is the subject of a
debate carried on by the university young people, posing the
question whether in moral terms the better-educated group is any
more worthy than the honest and level-headed but unlettered
Hannah, and whether in fact "civilizing" on their terms would
improve her.

An amusing tale and a thoroughly admirable heroine make the
Durket Sperret one of the best of Sada's local-color pieces. When
asked by the editors of *Book News* to comment upon this book, Sada
Elliott replied modestly:

I do not think that conscientiously I can claim any special purpose for

"The Durket Sperret." It came to me and so I wrote it. Having lived most of my life at Sewanee, the people are well known to me, and no one can know them without being struck by the pride of family which goes down through every grade of life, and consequently, with that conservative self-satisfaction which is the legitimate child of family pride, and which looks on progress as almost a sin, and change of any kind, as extremely pernicious. . . . But truly, the people were interesting to me, and in "The Durket Sperret," I hoped to make them interesting to others.[18]

A *New York Evening Post* review commended the character studies in *The Durket Sperret*, especially the homespun heroine and the termagant old grandmother, and concurred that the best scene in the book is the "buryin' " of Dave Durket. The reviewer thought the putting down of Si Durket well handled, and he rightly pointed out that "the author writes of her mountaineers with discrimination born of intimate knowledge. Too often they are treated . . . without regard to the social gulfs that may yawn between the dwellers in a Cumberland cove."[19] A *Charleston News and Courier* reviewer also noted that "as a sketch of life in the Tennessee mountains it is far more truly realistic than are the highly colored pictures of Charles Egbert Craddock (M. N. Murfree)." [20]

Two further stories, published at wide intervals, also utilized the characteristics of mountain people as plot elements: "A Little Child Shall Lead Them" and "Old Mrs. Dally's Lesson." The first was written expressly for the Christmas 1902 issue of *Youth's Companion*. As a seasonal offering it leans heavily on the reader's emotions, a melodramatic tale of a crippled child who saves her father from ambush in a mountain vendetta brought on a decade before by the illegal placement of a rail fence. Of all the mountain tales it is the easiest to read, because for some reason it was not written in dialect. The second story is somewhat related in theme in that it shows again the mountaineer's resistance to change.[21] Pictures of the marvels to be seen at the Centennial Exposition of 1876 attract the central character, old Mrs. Dally, and cause her to want to attend the event. For a year she works and saves until she can take her grandson on a trip to Nashville, her first journey outside the mountain valley in her entire life. When they arrive at the Exposition, she and Jim are bewildered and finally overwhelmed by all the new objects and experiences they encounter. An old spinning wheel in one display reminds Mrs. Dally of home, and she begins to realize what the security of her own home and way of life mean to her. She is grateful for the welcome she receives upon her return, and tells of her confusion at seeing so many newfangled machines and gadgets and other signs of technological progress. She apologizes for her restlessness and discontent, saying she is happier with the old ways.

The final use made of the mountain setting and characters was in "Moonshine Whiskey," a one-act tragedy, copyrighted May 16, 1912, and performed at least once in a pirated version given in California.[22] It, too, has a melodramatic scene in which Luella, the daughter of a moonshiner, sacrifices herself to prevent bloodshed, this time preventing her father's gunfire from killing Longley, a deputized revenue officer who comes to arrest him. Jarnigin, the father, has long been accustomed to making home-brewed whiskey, as did his Scotch-Irish ancestors, and stubbornly refuses to listen to reasons why under the new laws the revenuers must prevent him from selling it to make a living for his large family. The play is too brief for adequate character development, and little can be said for it except that actors would have no problem with the Southern mountain dialect, for once again it is carefully and almost phonetically spelled out.

IV *"The Fight for Truth"*: John Paget

In the middle of this regional phase of Elliott's work came a novel that defies easy classification, for although it contains regional elements, its concerns go beyond those which usually occupied the purely regional writer. *John Paget,* published by Henry Holt in 1893 on the heels of Elliott's success with *Jerry,* attempts to depict the prevailing values of two sections of the country. Like *The Felmeres,* it takes up many of the religious and moral questions of the day. Unfortunately, the arguments about current problems and what constitutes the good life are stated in a regional context which ultimately weakens them, since all the "good" characters come from the South and all the "bad" characters reside in the North, giving the book a sectional bias which, even if unintended, damages its credibility.

The opening chapters of *John Paget* are laid in the same Carolina low country locale used in the short story "Some Data," discussed earlier. The narrative begins in the middle of a dispute between Claudia Van Kuyster, who has just returned home after several years' absence, and her cousin Carter Wilton, a clergyman, once her fiancé. The quarrel concerns custody of two orphaned boys, John and Claude Paget, for whom Wilton has been made guardian following the war-related death of their father. Childless since her marriage to a wealthy Northern industrialist, Claudia agrees to adopt one of the boys, her namesake, Claude. The other brother, John, is taken to Texas and reared by Carter Wilton himself. What becomes of the two boys of identical inheritance when brought up in different environments—one in wealth, the other in genteel poverty—is the burden of the plot.

John Paget proceeds by means of the nature-versus-nurture argument to examine two value systems: the pursuit of happiness through wealth and ease, of "life as a picnic," versus the pursuit of personal meaning and worth through a life of service to one's fellow man. The Northern brother, Claude, having inherited his step-father's wealth, has been reared without any religious convictions and believes that "whatever is pleasant is right."[23] He is an atheist and a hedonist. Elliott makes him represent a godless and self-serving wealthy class associated with the "unwholesome" industrial metropolis. The other twin, John Paget, growing up in the postwar South and the frontier country of Texas, is a child of hardship. He represents Elliott's interpretation of the Southern experience: he is touched by suffering, poverty, sickness, and the harsh realities of having to fight for survival. Upon recovering from a serious illness, he dedicates himself to the alleviation of suffering and ignorance among his fellow men. As a ministerial student John Paget becomes a saintly figure, working in the slums of the city among the poor and sick. He denounces both society preachers and slum landlords and their indifference to the plight of the immigrant slum dwellers. When a yellow-fever epidemic breaks out in Texas he is drawn partly by the suffering reported there and partly by a sense of loyalty to a former sweetheart to leave the city and joint the fever fighters. John Paget's zeal and uncompromising honesty become an unspoken rebuke to the godless materialism and hedonism of his brother Claude, representing Elliott's notion of the Northerner's experience.

Both men have fallen in love with their convent-reared cousin Beatrice, Carter Wilton's only child. She is forced to choose between them. Claude attempts to persuade her to marry him and enjoy a life of ease and pleasure. John declares in a letter that he will make no claims upon her, for she must be free to make her own choice in love as well as in religious matters. The victim in this struggle between two attitudes toward life is the innocent Beatrice.

Warned by her tutor that Claude is persuading her to doubt her Christian faith, she decides that though she adores him she cannot give up her faith. Finally she runs away from the Van Kuysters, becomes lost while searching for John Paget in the midst of the epidemic, and dies of yellow fever.

The many shifts of scene and complicated family relationships, overly didactic conversations on theology, and the loosely connected romantic subplot fail to convince the reader despite the author's undoubted sincerity of purpose. It reveals, as *The Felmeres* had done, the depth of Elliott's religious convictions. It also reflects her belief that the South had much to teach the rest of the nation about human values.

The opening chapters, set in the Reconstruction South, echo some of Sada's own experiences, expressed in letters dating from this period. For example, Claudia Van Kuyster is warned by her cousin to watch out for roving bands of strange Negroes who do not belong on the place. At the same time she is concerned about the servants who have remained with the family, the house servants who must share their poverty. The old nurse Tenah expresses her feelings for the family thus: "Who I got in dis wull 'sides you an' Mass Cahter an' Mass Johnny chillun? Fahder in heben, *who* I got?" (10).

Claudia walks about the old house she once knew well and then strolls down to the boat landing to gaze out across the river: "how wide—how wide it was to the faraway dim line of woods on the other shore! And between the blues of wood and water, the low stretch of brown rice fields, with a storm house standing in the midst like a sentinel. The blue sky shone and sparkled as one looked, and the sunlight fell in a deluge of glory" (6). Her own former life seems to lie on the other side of that wide gulf. She now leads a hothouse existence away from the real sun and wind, underscored by the presence of a hothouse conservatory in her New York home. She is cut off not only from light and life but from any emotions as well. Claudia explains, "I stopped thinking and feeling some time ago. And when you harangue me on these subjects, I have a pre-existent sensation as it were; just as they say that after a man's leg has been cut off, he can still feel it, and have a shadow rheumatism in it" (262). Her lack of feeling stems from loneliness and disillusionment. Having chosen a life of wealth and ease over marriage to a poor clergyman, she is troubled by what her adopted son has become:

"You are sorry for me? . . . Do you suppose I am sensitive still? It would not be possible. I have sounded so many depths that I have reached the point where life seems a farce" (119).

Set opposite her disillusionment, typical of an unbelieving age, is the earnest faith of John Paget. To his New York relatives he appears an anachronism: "My dear John, you should have lived a thousand years ago; today you are an anomaly, you are a phenomenon that only the remotest provinces could have produced. That you should come to light in this age of 'isms,' and smooth words and ways, is almost enough to make one believe in miracles" (147-48).

While John is obsessed by the unhappy real present and the human conditions in the slums, Claudia is obsessed with the past. The smell of opopanax trees in blossom recalls her life in the old South and how it contrasted with her present existence:

How plainly she heard the waves and the wind that stirred in the opopanax trees outside the windows; she reached out and gathered the little yellow balls; how sweet they were! . . . How merrily the fire had crackled; how nice the lightwood had smelled as it burned—how blue the sky was; how sweet the orange blossoms that looked in at the open window! How oppressive the steady heat of the Northern houses had been to her, after the open windows and roaring fires of her home! The careless, spendthrift, comfortable, arrogant, beautiful South—what a wonderful life the "upper ten thousand" had led—how sure they had been that the world had been made for them! Swept away! And now it was becoming a money-making, and money-saving, conventional country like any other. (76)

Somewhere amid Claudia's nostalgia for the South and its lost way of life and the search for certainty in a doubting age the book falters. Hab Elliott had once said his sister would preach to thousands. In this book she is in the pulpit a good bit of the time, and the text of her sermon is "A luxurious, unbelieving age—grant it. But there has never been an age when men were more eager for the truth—when men were more earnestly pleading for some firm place where they could cling; never an age when humanity was so eager to help humanity; never an age when people cried out more for reality! It seems to me that there never has been a grander age in which to make the fight for truth!" (128) One cannot find fault with the author for having tried to present her view of The Truth, the view that Christian concern and faith still have value in a doubting age and are to be valued more highly than riches. However, the plot seems

melodramatic and contrived, and the characters are either too good
or too bad to be convincing. They are essentially embodied arguments.

Writing this book was probably a sublimation of Elliott's intention
to produce a biography of her brother, for there are many striking
resemblances between the young priest of the novel and the bishop:
like Bishop Elliott, John Paget is shown as a saintly and unworldly
priest trying to lead a sincerely dedicated life. He castigates those
priests who avoid involvement with human suffering. Bishop Elliott, as a young man, served in New York as assistant at the Church
of the Incarnation, where he ministered to the city's poor as John
Paget does in the novel. In real life he had been offered but had
refused a call to more than one wealthy parish, for he was a man of
great personal charm and a gifted preacher, but he had chosen
instead the more difficult calling of missionary. The work was poorly
paid, physically demanding, and often hazardous; he had contracted
malaria and had experienced yellow-fever epidemics. Thus Elliott
seems to have endowed her hero with many of her brother's
experiences, traits, and beliefs, shared also by their father, to whose
memory the work is dedicated.

V Sam Houston

A knowledge of Texas and a familiarity with its history became of
real benefit when in 1900 Elliott was asked to undertake a biography
of a fellow Tennessean, Sam Houston. The work was one of a series
of biographies, the Beacon Biographies of Eminent Americans,
designed, according to the editors, for "the average busy man and
woman who have not the time or hardly the inclination to acquaint
themselves with American biography" (144). It was published by
Small, Maynard in 1900, a tiny volume of 144 pages.

Maligned and slandered by his numerous political opponents,
Sam Houston was in need of "rehabilitation" as a frontier hero. The
South, moreover, needed to be reminded of its heroes neglected
since the Civil War. Elliott was able to bring in new material
obtained from Elihu Chauncey, a New York friend, and Judge John
M. Lea of Nashville, which explained why Houston abandoned his
wife, suddenly resigned as Governor of Tennessee, and left for the
Texas territory shortly after his marriage. It had been revealed later
by his second wife that he had married a woman who did not love

him and that by apparently abandoning her he left the way open for divorce. This was but one episode of many in which the reckless vigor of his character was to cause him to be criticized, bringing him as many enemies as he had admirers.

Elliott expressed once in a book review how she thought a biography should be written: "opening with some striking act or scene of later date when the hero has become really interesting and then, if necessary, going back to the milk-bottle, the perambulator, the capable housekeeping grandmother, and the grandfather who liked, and who would have a good horse."[24] This is how she wrote the Sam Houston biography, beginning with an overview of his career and citing a crucial point in it when he refused in 1861 to lead Texas, after its annexation, out of the Union again into Secession. Elliott could sympathize with Houston's divided loyalty over this issue, even while his son enlisted to fight for the Southern cause. Her own family members had had mixed feelings over the wisdom of Secession, and their forward-looking liberalism had often come in contact with the reactionary Southern majority.

After cursory mention of the subject's early life, Elliott covers his contact with the Cherokees, his army career and lifelong friendship with Andrew Jackson, his work in behalf of the Indians in Texas and how he became a member of one tribe and took a native wife. The battle for independence is swiftly painted as are the political years as president of the territory, then as governor and senator; many important events are only mentioned in passing, for Elliott found it difficult to compress so eventful a life into "so brief a space," calling it but a sketch of the man.

She demonstrates her fondness for the Texas landscape by painting it as a vivid backdrop for the fast-sweeping events of Houston's life. She introduces dialogue and many quotations to make the historic figures seem to live and move. As a local colorist, she also emphasizes certain Southern traits in Houston's character; his recklessness and passionate temper, which led him into a duel and a charge of caning a member of Congress (for which he was tried and fined); his eloquence and magnetism as a leader; his humor and backwoods folksiness; and his habit of whittling small wooden toys as he sat listening to long-winded speeches in the Senate.

Elliott does not shy away from the slavery issues involved in the annexation question, but neither does she linger long over political questions, choosing instead to enlarge the reader's sympathy for the man who "spent the best years of his life in this work, had endured obloquy and physical suffering in the doing; and now, old and poor, he was put aside while his work was undone" (141).

As a group, the regional pieces, the novel of ideas *John Paget*, and the Houston biography are uneven in quality, as we have seen. The four or five short stories in *An Incident and Other Happenings*, written at the height of Elliott's powers, and showing a careful matching of subject and method, are probably her best. Commenting upon this collection in a critical essay on Elliott for *The Library of Southern Literature* (1907), B. Lawton Wiggins concurred in this judgment: "The artistic handling, the reticence, the condensation, the delicate pathos, the clear vision of character in these stories . . . are the best work the author has yet done" (1555).

CHAPTER 4

Problems of the New South

PROGRESS was the catch word of Southern economic recovery after 1876. Slowly farmers moved away from single-crop agriculture; lumber and mineral resources were exploited; railway construction was begun. New railroads and steel mills created a demand for coal, causing a coal-mining boom in Kentucky and West Virginia. Cheap labor and abundant waterpower brought the first textile mills to towns that lay at the fall lines of Southern rivers. Henry W. Grady of Atlanta and N. G. Gonzales of Columbia eagerly promoted further progress in their editorial columns.

But progress was slow in coming and it did not reach everyone: Negroes were newly disfranchised by Jim Crow laws; children worked as long as fourteen hours in the cotton mills; coal miners worked in hazardous mine shafts. Sharecropping continued to be the way of life for most farmers. The newfound wealth that poured into the South seemed to fall into only a few hands. Soon the prevailing doctrine of an industrial society—every man for himself—came to be understood in the easygoing South. What was worse, the Populist leaders who promised salvation often turned out to be political opportunists or demagogues.

Out of this welter of economic and social problems came Sarah Elliott's most popular novel, *Jerry*, a story of Southerners transplanted to a Western mining town, presumably in the Boulder-Denver area of Colorado, where a major gold rush was underway in the 1860s and 1870s. Gold mining meant rapid wealth, and this sudden wealth became Elliott's vehicle for an analysis of materialism and the abuses of the period of the Agrarian Revolt. Similar problems were experienced in the coal-mining towns of the East: railway construction was accompanied by land speculation; gold and coal mining encouraged stock speculation; fortunes were made and lost in a day.

But these were not the only problems of the New South Elliott

examined in her stories. What interested her most was the impact of
the new values on veterans and small businessmen and farmers.
There was the ever-present Negro Question and the problem of
asking the nonvoting black man to serve his country in the war with
Spain. Furthermore, with all its new problems, the South still
suffered many of its former ills; there remained vestiges of the old
Code Duello as well as lynching and mob violence. After 1900
Elliott turned from fiction to direct examination of such current
problems as woman's suffrage and labor disputes and helped to edit
a quarterly review which featured many of these issues.

Progress is a necessary evil, Elliott seems to say, but the South is
paying for it in a lost sense of community. Materialism is driving out
old values but adding few graces to life. And the old vices persist:
greed, violence, false pride, unreasoning prejudice, and antiintellectualism, which stifle creativity and deny social justice. And still
more than half the South's citizens remain powerless at the ballot
box.

I   *"New People to Fight New Times"*

A real break in Elliott's career came in 1888, with the acceptance
of one of her stories, "An Ex-brigadier," by *Harper's Monthly*, one
of the most widely read magazines of the day. Not only was
publication by *Harper's* an important sign of professional recognition, but the story itself was to be the first of several stories and a
major novel in which Elliott focused on the problems of the New
South.

The setting for "An Ex-brigadier" is a small Alabama town, a town
which local inhabitants hope will turn into a metropolis as soon as
the railway comes through. The narrator, Willoughby, is a representative of a New York railway syndicate who has come to town to spy
out good land purchases for construction of the railway. He introduces himself to the leading man of the town, General Billy
Stamper, a boyhood friend of Willoughby's father. During a visit to
the rundown residence of General Billy, Willoughby is regaled,
over homemade whiskey, with the old man's adventures as an
itinerant preacher, a profession he took up after losing a leg in the
war. In the struggle to survive the economic depression of the 1870s
many Southerners had to sacrifice their principles, the general
explains. "We have lost the art of being satisfied," he goes on. "We

are learning to be avaricious, for now in the South position is coming to depend on money; so all grind along together; and I hate it."[1]

The story's basic theme is one of changing values. Billy Stamper, the former planter turned itinerant preacher, sees himself as a virtual confidence man. He has tried to change with the harsh economic winds and is now living on land speculation—a trade he would formerly have despised. When the young railway agent protests that he cannot take advantage of his friendship with General Billy to advance the railway company's interest, Billy points out that this is " 'Befo' de wah' sensitiveness which we cannot afford now—"(888). Billy Stamper has become a man of the new age; inborn gentility has no market value anymore; he cannot afford the luxury of being sensitive about his source of income.

There is some hint at the end of the story that the railway agent does manage to bring profit to the ex-brigadier and the small Alabama town. Thus it is implied that, despite the changing values of the time, friendship and common links with a gentle past still have some meaning.

The character sketch of General Billy and his irrepressible will to survive makes "An Ex-brigadier" one of Elliott's best stories. Its subject and its setting in the Reconstruction South were timely and marked a welcome shift from subjects like travel and Americans abroad to more contemporary topics, such as economic recovery. It was followed by a group of stories concerned with the recent past and the South's struggles to come to terms with the ethics of the marketplace.

Progress, the rallying cry of the promoters and politicos of the New South, was, as C. Vann Woodward has shown, the all-consuming interest of Southern editors and businessmen, yeoman and aristocrat alike. Mercantile enterprises of every kind were springing up. New types of manufactures were being attempted, along with railway expansion, mining, lumbering, and shipping, and these resulted in the growth of Southern hamlets into towns and cities.[2] But the feeling persisted among many Southerners that progress was being made at the expense of human values. The victim of progress was often a small-town farmer-turned-merchant who lacked either the know-how, the drive, or the capital to make his business successful. It was the opportunist, the man of few scruples, who would triumph, like Faulkner's much-chronicled Snopes family.

This idea about the dubious blessings of progress was expressed in an Elliott story entitled simply "Progress," which appeared in *McClure's Magazine* (November 1899). Sam Long, unlike Billy Stamper of "An Ex-brigadier," has found that the rapid changes of the 1880s have brought him nothing but trouble. In spite of the general expansion and economic upturn, Sam is bankrupt. Ten years before, he had sold some of his farmland to the new railway line. Now at the corner of his old field a railway station and post office have been built. Soon a physician builds a small office on another piece of Sam's land, and bit by bit the town of Longville springs up to serve the farmers in the surrounding countryside. Sam's wife opens a boarding house to which the doctor frequently brings his patients for dinner, and Sam opens a general store to further accommodate his neighbors.

Now Sam finds that the grand new era of prosperity has been a mixed blessing, increasing everyone's craving for store-bought things while leaving little time to enjoy them. Mrs. Long's boarding house has lost money because she will never turn anyone away hungry, whether or not he can pay. Sam has stocked his store by mortgaging his house and remaining land, but his customers, always short on cash and long on credit, seldom pay. Soon he has so many debts he is about to lose his home—financially ruined, as he sees it, by progress. Too kindhearted to make his neighbors pay up, he has been cheated by even his best friends. The unbusinesslike Sam and his attorney Abe Hicks go to break the news to his mother that they must give up the home place. More stoic and wise than any of them, the old woman is fully prepared for the news they bring: she shows them the small horde of money and handmade goods she has put by in the event of such a crisis. "It takes new people to fight new times," the old lady observes. They will rebuild on a small piece of land she owns in the hills and start over again, leaving progress to those who are "knowing enough and hard enough to wrestle with it."[3]

Though published a decade apart, "An Ex-brigadier" and "Progress" share the theme of change and an agrarian culture's coming to terms with commerce. Each is an unspoken plea for salvaging from the Southern experience certain humane values, such as the close-knit community of family and friends who sustain and support one another in good times as well as bad. Elliott harbored an abiding concern that material progress might wipe out this strong sense of community interdependence, the liberality and enjoyment of each other's company that is at the heart of the Southerner's sense of hospitality. She felt that loss of these values would be worse than economic disaster. Her prophetic concern was echoed manyfold in 1930 by the writer-scholars of *I'll Take My Stand.*[4]

The South would slowly recover from its economic lethargy and learn to cope with progress, but the nation still viewed the region with suspicion. The Negro problem was far from solved, and if anything had been worsened by grandfather clauses and poll-tax laws which effectively disfranchised blacks and many illiterate whites. Old resentments left over from the Civil War were still smoldering as long as thirty years later. Could blacks achieve full citizenship in the South? The nation wanted to know.

In 1898 Sada Elliott was so caught up by the issues of the war with Spain that she tried in every way for an opportunity to write about it firsthand by going to Cuba as a correspondent. She recognized that the South's involvement with the war would be of interest to national magazines. She wrote a story dealing with both questions: the loyalty of Southerners in a national conflict, and the position of blacks in the war effort. "Hands All Round" (*Book News,* September 1898) takes up the question of the South's loyalty: will its men fight side by side with soldiers from other parts of the country in the war against Spain, or will sectional feeling prevent them from demonstrating their full citizenship?

The story begins with a capsule history of an upcountry Southern town, Atlanta or Columbia, perhaps, here called Preston. Preston has suffered devastation in the "War of Secession" and has slowly pulled itself up from defeat and bankruptcy to a precarious prosperity. Faced by the Cuban question, the Preston Greys militia, led by Francis Newman (a new manner of man, as his name implies), must decide whether their company will join the general call for volunteers, to side with the Liberty and Progress party, or whether they will support the conservative Peace party. "Go to Cuba to fight for half-castes," they scoff, "to die of yellow fever. Francis Newman was crazy, it *should not be!*"[5]

The town is thrown into a state of shock when it is learned that, following this rebuff, Francis has had a meeting with the Negro citizens of the town, at their request, to organize a volunteer company for the Spanish War. An officer arrives and blacks begin to enlist in their own volunteer corps. A town meeting is held to debate the issue of peace or war. The opposition is led by Captain Alderley, father of Francis Newman's fiancée, Ann. He rises to

speak against sending "our sons to a war that does not concern us."
Francis Newman retaliates with arguments for freedom for Cuba
and the Philippines, "for the world is looking to us to share the
blessings of liberty to all . . . and the blood on the battlefields is
all of one hue!" Francis wins over the members of the corps of
Greys, and even Ann Alderley promises she will wait for his return
from war in spite of her divided loyalty.

The timeliness of the issues and the swift, clear narration in
"Hands All Round" show that over three decades Elliott had indeed
come to master the art she had practiced so diligently since 1870.
She now had a knack for subjects and a sure grasp of popular
storytelling techniques.

Other aspects of the race issue continued to be a problem in the
New South. In an age without welfare legislation, who was responsible for the aged and destitute, especially those of the black race?
Those who had "old ties" of respect and affection continued to
assume what responsibility they could, despite their own economic
hardships. Even more than financial aid, some form of personal
interest and protection often meant the difference between life and
death for the individual in need. Such is the case in an unpublished
story called "Old Ties," in which Elliott describes the relationship
between Selwyn, a none-too-prosperous planter of the postwar
years, and his former nurse, named Lucy, now old and sick and in
need of friends. Another aged black woman named Myra, with a
reputation for having "the evil eye" and the ability to work magic
spells in order to prey on her own people, has victimized Lucy, sold
off her household goods, and all but starved her to death. When this
situation is brought to Selwyn's attention, he threatens to send Myra
to jail for her cruelty and dishonesty. Lucy is rescued and brought
home to Selwyn's farm, where she can be cared for properly.

Miscegenation is the subject of two other unpublished stories, "A
Speculation in Futures" and "The Heart of It." The subject of mixed
blood was still largely taboo during Elliott's lifetime, however, and
she was unable to find a publisher for these stories. It would be
another quarter of a century before Faulkner would introduce in
fiction the white McCaslins and their brethren, the black and white
half-brothers of *Absalom, Absalom!* and Joe Christmas of *Light in
August*. In both of Elliott's stories a young man or woman of mixed
blood has been reared in a white family and learns as an adult that
he or she may not marry the person of his or her choice. Miscegenation laws, which prevented and still prevent such marriages in some

Southern states, would have to be invoked, along with the unwritten laws of the Color Line. In each case, Elliott handled the material with sympathy for the individuals of mixed parentage, recognizing the personal tragedy such discoveries entailed. While she dared to write on such "touchy" subjects, she could not find a publisher for them, but left them as a kind of legacy to remind others of the complexity of the problems faced by the South in the postwar years.

II *"Every Man for Himself"*: Jerry

Coming to terms with an industrial age had occupied Elliott's thoughts for some years. She at last embodied her concerns in a novel, about which she wrote to several editors in 1887 while traveling in Europe. She told one editor that she had been working on a longer serial of some 500 foolscap pages which might interest him and which she thought was better than her most recently published novelette, *A Simple Heart*. She asked him to place it for her if he could and sent along a copy of *The Felmeres* as a gentle reminder of what she was capable of doing with a longer work.

With the publication of "An Ex-brigadier" in *Harper's*, Elliott had gained entrance into the national magazines, and there was a better chance than ever for acceptance of the longer manuscript. *Scribner's* eventually bought the serial rights, and *Jerry* began a year-long serialization (June 1890 to May 1891). The novel was also accepted for book publication by Henry Holt.

After reading the first two installments of *Jerry* in *Scribner's*, Thomas Nelson Page, then unofficial dean of Southern writers, wrote from London to bestow congratulations upon the author. What praise he gave can only be guessed, for this story did not deal in any way with the Old South. *Jerry* was a product of the New South, concerned with mining and the effects of railway expansion, the growth of towns, and schemes for redistribution of wealth that sprang up during the period of Populist politics (1880-1892). Strictly speaking, *Jerry* is not even a regional novel. Its characters are Southerners transplanted from their native Kentucky and Tennessee to the West, although they carry with them their regional attitudes about honor, trade, and fair dealing (along with their difficult-to-read local dialects). The novel tries to speak of economic problems which beset not just the South but many parts of the country, an indication that the author had deliberately tried to choose national themes.

Although Elliott's reply to Page traded on their mutual Southern traits, there is more than a little "tongue in cheek" to her remarks about where Page stood with Southerners, and where *she* now stood—for, after all, *Jerry* had made it in the *world*, not the South alone:

> I am very glad that the world seems to think so well of "Jerry"—I assure you that his mother has had him put away for some time, not thinking that he had "legs enough" to "go it alone." (Two dreadful phrases, which you will please hide in the recesses of your fire.) More than all, I am glad that *you* think well of him. You ought to know where you and "Mars Chan" and "Meh Lady" stand with all Southern people. The world crowns you, and well it may, but your own people hold you in their hearts—and so your commendation is much—very much to me.[6]

Jerry contains many elements current in regional and local-color fiction in the 1880s: a runaway boy with a thick hill-country accent who might have stepped out of one of Mary Noailles Murfree's mountain tales, and a haunted gold mine not unlike the cave in *Tom Sawyer*.[7] But there are other elements that look beyond local color to the economic novels of the next three decades. A main character who becomes a popular labor reformer prefigures such characters as Annixter of Norris's *The Octopus* (1901) or young Conrad Dryfoos of Howells's earlier *A Hazard of New Fortunes* (1889), and the prominence of gold suggests Norris's *McTeague* (1899).

Indeed, the use of gold as a symbol of the mercenary Gilded Age is a significant feature of *Jerry*. The power of gold to corrupt even the most dedicated of men is a necessary element of motivation. Others, such as George Eliot in *Silas Marner*, had used gold before for such a purpose. Eight years after *Jerry*, Norris also would use gold in *McTeague* to represent the effect of greed on the simple-minded dentist who is goaded by his wife's acquisitiveness into ever-widening circles of moral corruption.

At the beginning it is not gold but grief and guilt which drive Jeremiah Wilkerson, the hero Jerry, out of his Cumberland mountain home into the world west of the mountains. A small boy brutalized by a drunken father, reviled and beaten by a new stepmother, Jerry runs away to save his life. Still stunned by the death and hasty burial of his mother, Jerry goes to find her, thinking she has gone westward on a long journey. He stows away on a train and a steamboat which take him farther and farther from his home. At last he stumbles into a mining town somewhere in the western mountains, referred to as "Durden's" throughout the story, where he is adopted by a gold prospector. The prospector, a former Kentuckian named Joe Gilliam, recognizes the boy's origins by his dialect.

The local medical doctor is an Easterner who has chosen this unlikely place to hide from the world and rear his nephew and ward, Paul Henley. The physician succeeds in drawing Jerry's mind away from his obsessive guilt about his mother's death and begins to educate the boy. Soon the doctor becomes not only Jerry's teacher but also his exemplar and hero. Ten years pass, during which Joe Gilliam cares for the boy's physical wants while the doctor teaches him sufficiently well for Jerry to become the town schoolmaster.

Dismayed at the poverty and ignorance of the people he instructs, Jerry devises a plan for their economic salvation through revitalizing Durden's Mine. The mine has had a strange history. Indians who had once brought gold from it had fled into it to avoid being massacred; they perished when they fell into a deep, hidden chasm, and their deaths placed a curse upon the mine—a curse so forbidding that no one in recent time except Durden and his partner Lije Milton had been known to venture there. In actuality, Joe Gilliam had fostered the legend of the haunted mine to hide the fact that he had discovered its richest vein. Daily he crossed the forbidding chasm to reach his secret hoard. Earlier owners had built a coffer-dam upstream from the mine to divert the water from a river that flowed underground into the mine. If the cofferdam were not carefully maintained, the underground river would return to its old channel and flood the mine.

The people of Eureka, a nearby mining town, are competing with Durden's for the railway line which is moving westward across the prairies. Jerry has persuaded the townspeople of Durden's to buy shares in the old mine and reopen it for commercial operation. Next he must see to it that the railway line coming to Eureka is brought as far as Durden's. Preaching the evils of land speculation, he warns the townspeople not to sell to the railway speculators but to hold their land for sale at a fair price to newcomers who will be attracted by the reopening of the mine. A mysterious buyer, revealed to be none other than the doctor, Jerry's former teacher, has been acquiring large tracts in the center of the village. There is much resentment and misunderstanding at the discovery.

Jerry decides to go back East to convince the major stockholders that his town and mine are sound investments. Joe Gilliam, mean-

while, has decided to leave Jerry his hidden fortune in gold but fears
that Jerry will not value it and will give it all away. Joe determines to
use Jerry's trip as a way to teach him to appreciate all that money
can buy. He writes ahead that Jerry is to be given unlimited credit
to spend as much as he likes.

By a series of rapid transformations, Jerry has become a persuasive speaker, a dedicated labor leader, and now a capitalist. Back
East, he learns to enjoy his newfound wealth and importance as he
models himself after the doctor and his influential friends. Gradually
his selfless concern for organizing the miners into a commune fades
as he discovers the lure of even greater wealth that he might obtain
through stock speculation.

Paul Henley, the doctor's ward, is Jerry's social and business
rival. Paul looks down on Jerry, the self-made man, and is contemp-
tuous of his efforts to improve the economic lot of the working class,
with which Jerry continues to identify.

When Joe Gilliam's death brings Jerry a fortune in gold, previ-
ously hidden in the rafters of the prospector's cabin, Jerry invests all
his secret inheritance in Durden's Mine stock to tide the enterprise
over its period of development. His desire to outmaneuver Paul
Henley, together with his newfound materialism, make him a
changed man. A plan is devised to bring an excursion train along the
newly laid track to advertise the mining towns to prospective
settlers. Lured by half-fare rides, many take advantage of the cheap
holiday and the chance to view the quaint mountainfolk and their
frontier ways.

Jerry's mentor, the village doctor, receives a letter informing him
that his secret love, Paul Henley's mother, has died. Soon after, the
doctor either jumps or falls from a high rock into the valley below.
His will leaves all his property for a school and orphanage for the
mining town where he has lived for twenty years.

Gold fever and land speculation mount until newspapers back
East are daily publishing engineering reports on the mine, causing
Durden's stock to soar. Paul Henley persuades all the important
investors who join in the railway excursion to visit *his* mining town
of Eureka, sending only the pleasure seekers on to Durden's. Paul
at the same time fosters rumors that Jerry has secretly bought up all
Durden's stock and plans to sell out at a quick profit. The
townspeople turn on Jerry and in a drunken rage destroy the
cofferdam, unwittingly flooding Durden's and the lower Eureka

mine as well. Jerry, financially ruined, dies of the effects of the mob's violence.

More than once in *Jerry* Elliott comments on the materialism of the age: "Money bought love, and honor, and power, and friendship, and souls, and bodies; and the free and enlightened Nineteenth Century saw more slavery and subjection than any other age of the world."[8] The novel's central theme is the effect of materialism on individuals and groups, as shown in the attitudes of various characters toward gold. Joe Gilliam, the old prospector, has a simple-minded instinct to hoard, never spending his money except for the barest necessities. In a totally misguided effort to teach Jerry the value of money, he turns the schoolteacher's altruism to greed. Paul Henley, on the other hand, values money for the power it brings to control the lives of others. His guardian, the town doctor, also joins in land speculation, but the doctor's motives are basically philanthropic, since he leaves his land to the community. His Eastern friends buy stock in the mine and speculate in land as much for the sport as for profit. The ignorant miners, however, who have been persuaded to invest in the mine, do so for the hope of "striking it rich" and making better lives for themselves. They become involved in land price inflation, while Jerry causes stock price manipulations, two of the many economic abuses of the Gilded Age.

Despite these efforts to deal with contemporary economic problems, the book has many weak points. The sudden transition of an illiterate mountain boy into a well-read, gentlemanly hero of the people is barely plausible, and Jerry's second transition from hero of the people into ambitious speculator, a much overused fictional device in the Horatio Alger tradition, is even less believable.

Because *Jerry* deals with the evils of materialism and because the main character is corrupted by gold and brought to his doom by the onrush of seemingly inevitable forces, some critics have classified it as a naturalistic novel like Norris's *McTeague*, which it preceded by eight years. There are several interesting parallels between *Jerry* and *McTeague:* the brutalizing effect of greed, the dominant symbolism of gold, together with scenes in a gold mine, and two strikingly similar scenes in which main characters literally worship the sight and touch of large amounts of gold. But Elliott was not a Naturalist.

She was thoroughly familiar with the literary techniques of the

Naturalist, and with the Naturalist's belief that, given only a man's natural endowments and his upbringing, one could almost predict his fate. She did not agree with this deterministic attitude toward life. While utilizing some of the stylistic techniques of the Naturalist, she tried to show in her stories and novels that the option for personal choice was always open, and that human beings need not follow blindly some inner gyroscope set to guide the individual into inevitable despair.

Elliott makes her central character Jerry bring about his own downfall because he becomes a man of his age—a rugged individualist who forgets to love his fellow man. She chastises him in biblical images that her father might have chosen: "This man whose power was bound to increase because daily he was learning the motto of the Age—'Every man for himself.' If every man stop to help his brother; to 'pour oil and wine' and bring him to a safe resting-place, who could first reach the goal? Who could do more than win food and raiment, if this were the code? The creed of individualism can permit no such weakness as this; the narrower the aim, the harder the heart, the surer the success!" (393). Indeed, like the typical self-made man of the age, Jerry begins to suffer from the chronic ailment, "Hardness of Heart," the occupational illness of misers. "His heart hardened within him: what use to love or trust?" Sada asks (354). Nurture by a gruff but loving stepfather and by a wise teacher has done much for Jerry, but cannot do all things. He betrays his upbringing through an inordinate love of wealth and power, corrupted not by his genes but by his own moral choices. He has been led to these choices in part by the dominant ethic of the day—Social Darwinism—survival of the fittest in the competitive business world. He has been thrust unprepared into a world where old values, old faiths are being driven out by science and industrial progress. He is a true child of the South, reared by a Kentucky backwoodsman whose values were not of this hard "Iron Age." Jerry has been overwhelmed by the Social Darwinism of the Machine Age:

This proud, hard Nineteenth Century that vaunts itself that it neither fears nor loves—that glories in tearing the veil from the "Holy of Holies" that the mob might be as free to touch and see as the "Anointed of the Lord"! that analyzes every throb of brain and heart; that laughs faith and hope to scorn, holding only certainty: that shuts charity into hospital wards: that teaches the "survival of the fittest"; that tests prayer and crowds down the weak and the poor to death and annihilation. Hailing "labor-saving" inventions with a shout of triumph, and trusting to disease and death to clear the overcrowded garrets and cellars!

Clamoring and battling for gold; and legislating on the crowded prisons and lunatic asylums! This great "Iron Age" that has no heart save the thud of machinery—is this the music it dances to?

. . . Do we hear the heart of the Nineteenth Century pulsing in its music—the saddest music the world has ever heard? (274)

To his credit, Jerry briefly tries to alleviate the hardships of the people of Durden by organizing them into a commune, but the effort is shortlived—the people become discontented and suspicious of their leader, and rebel. This socialist answer to the widening economic gulf between classes that accompanied the expansionist years resembles the utopian society of Edward Bellamy's *Looking Backward* (1888) and Howells's *Traveler from Altruria* (1894). Upton Sinclair would also search for a socialist's answer later in *The Jungle* (1906). But Jerry has little success establishing a worker-owned gold mine at Durden's among the illiterate and fiercely independent populace, and in the end mob violence destroys both the leader and the source of wealth itself—the mine.

Throughout the South and Middle West, uprisings of farmers and other victims of economic exploitation became the Agrarian Revolt, giving rise to such groups as the Farmers' Alliance and the People's Party, the Populist movement of the 1890s. This banding-together of little men to oppose the landlords and industrial robber barons was chronicled by both Western and Southern realists. Marion Lack, whose master's thesis explores the phenomenon of the Agrarian Revolt as reflected in the fiction of the 1880s and 1890s, notes that there were some twenty-four authors and fifty novels published by 1900 which touched on the revolt of the working classes.[9] Of these, only three Southerners other than Mark Twain examined in their novels the economic problems of the period with any real discernment: George Washington Cable, James Lane Allen, and Sarah Barnwell Elliott. Lack attributes the general apathy of the Southern writers to a combination of factors, including the strength of the railroad and monied interests, the almost hope-less economic prostration of the South as a whole, and the timidity of the authors themselves in pinpointing through fiction all the economic abuses that existed.[10] New England writers as a group dealt with poverty in their farming regions, but they did not touch on such problems as land speculation, corruption and bribery in government, or railway construction and its attendant abuses. Middle Western novelists like Edward Eggleston, E. W. Howe, and Hamlin Garland were more sympathetic than the Southerners to the problems of the small farmers. Though the Southern writers did point out many of the abuses they saw, as a group they were generally not very effective in prompting their readers to work for lowering tariffs, discouraging wild speculations, regulating government corruption, or sponsoring welfare measures.

A liberal Democrat but no socialist or Populist, Elliott could not write with pure conviction on the subject of the Agrarian Revolt. In the South this movement took many forms, not all of them effective, and found many unlikely and none-too-trustworthy champions, such as the future Governor of South Carolina, Ben Tillman, whom Elliott despised. However, it is to her considerable credit that she attempted to deal with the economic wrongs of the day and brought forward a popular champion, Jerry, who attempts to alleviate them, making her novel a voice for reform a decade before James Lane Allen's *Reign of Law* (1900) and a quarter of a century before the work of T. S. Stribling, Ellen Glasgow, and William Faulkner.

Despite an overabundance of harangues against the godless materialism of the age and some weakness of plotting and character development, *Jerry* is an engrossing tale. The reader becomes involved in the struggles of the main character, his arduous climb upward, his efforts at reform, and his dramatic downfall. Contemporary readers of the 1890s must have found the story to their taste, for *Jerry* met with immediate nationwide success even before the hardback copies were in the bookstores. This time Elliott's critics centered their comments on the book's plot and the timely subject, instead of the parentage and background of the "charming authoress." The book was widely and generously reviewed in the national press, and editions were soon brought out in England, Germany, and Australia.

III   *Out-thinking the Present Needs*

More and more through the 1890s Elliott gave her attention to challenging problems of the New South, which was slowly beginning economic recovery. Yet many issues of the Progressive movement were unresolved: political disfranchisement of the Negro and poor whites, woman's rights, child-labor problems, vote fraud, working conditions in textile mills, and railway regulation, to name but a few.

Little if any frank public debate on these problems had been seen or heard in the Deep South since George Washington Cable had attempted to provide a forum for debate through his "Open Letter Club." Cable had begun in 1887 to distribute pamphlets written by himself and others on controversial questions relating to race, labor, education, and economics. None of these topics was easily publishable in Southern periodicals, and so the pamphlets formed a means of discussing them. They were to be sent on requests to subscribers of the "Open Letter Club," which was to include among its members educators and church and professional persons of liberal sentiments throughout the South. The idea for the club had originated soon after Cable lectured in 1887 at the Monteagle Assembly a few miles from Sewanee. In his speech, entitled "Cobwebs in the Church," Cable challenged the churches to free themselves of their exclusiveness and to enter into the affairs of the day. He especially urged free debate on the Negro Question—in effect, to practice what they preached! The idea for free exchange of views was a good one, but the club expired with the second symposium for lack of subscribers.[11]

Twenty years passed before a similar exchange of views took place in the South. On July 4, 1909, at the fifty-first Founders' Day celebration of the University of the South, 1858–1909, the university held a conference on "The South Today." Topics included Southern politics and economics, the long-range effects of Reconstruction, the Negro Question, railroad rates and their effect on commerce, labor problems, as well as education for women and the state of the arts. So controversial were some of the issues to be dealt with, even as late as 1909, that they could be openly discussed at all only because the participants were highly respected religious leaders. Even so, responses from many prominent persons to requests for papers ranged from amusement to indifference to flat refusal even to discuss the facts of the matter, much less their broader political implications.

Contributions *were* forthcoming, finally, and out of this stimulating conference came articles and papers of such breadth of insight that the participants agreed to find some way for them to be published and distributed. Thereupon the university created a quarterly review, the *Forensic Quarterly*, as the means of addressing a wider audience. Recognizing that the venture could expect no support from advertising, the editor arranged for the quarterly to be published under the aegis of the University Extension Program,

which conducted summer lecture series and offered syllabi of
courses for nonresident students. His opening editorial acknowledged that, while many of the subjects were controversial, "society
can grow only by the aid of such of her members as out-think the
present needs" and that without exercising the freedom to speak out
on such issues, society would stagnate.[12]

Since the original conference had been structured as a regional
survey, the papers offered in the *Forensic Quarterly* were regional
in outlook; but many authors also strove to place their Southern
themes within the broader context of national life. Some of the titles
in the first issue were "Political Solidarity in the South Today," by
Thomas Gailor, Bishop of Tennessee and Chancellor of the University; "Relation of the South to the Nation," by William Alexander
Guerry, Bishop of South Carolina; and several papers on the Negro
problem, one of which advocated broader Negro suffrage. In the
second issue, devoted mainly to the current status of women, there
were papers such as "The Effect on Woman of Economic Dependence," by Charles Zeublin; a description of the newly opened
Newcomb College for women in New Orleans; and articles on child
labor and on the arts in the South.

Sarah Barnwell Elliott contributed an essay entitled "A Study of
Woman and Civilization" to this second issue. The essay is a
tongue-in-cheek "history" of womankind, reminiscent of Margaret
Fuller's "Woman in the Nineteenth Century" but lighter in tone,
yet with the serious purpose of making a plea for suffrage for
women.

The third issue of the *Quarterly* carried a factual report by Elliott
entitled "An Epoch-Making Settlement Between Labor and
Capital."[13] This report was a compilation of letters, newspaper
reports, and official statements regarding the Cherry Mine disaster,
a coal-mine explosion and cave-in in Streator, Illinois, in November
1909, which had taken the lives of 270 miners and many rescue
workers. The epoch-making settlement spoken of was the ruling
that for the first time made mine owners accountable for the safety
of their workers and required that a workmen's compensation fund
be set up to indemnify the families of miners killed by the explosion.
For the first time in the history of American industry, so far as
Elliott knew, a labor group through a skilled mediator had successfully obtained workmen's compensation for injury or death along the
lines of the English Workman's Compensation Act of 1906. Quicker
than most to perceive the long-term implications of this decision,

Elliott wrote a lucid account of the settlement and its consequences. Demand for the article was so great that a separate reprint of it was issued by the University Press.

The masthead of the third issue of the *Forensic Quarterly* carried Sarah Barnwell Elliott's name as associate editor. Her influence had come to the fore with the second issue, and it remained in evidence in the form of book reviews and the choice of material that would be of interest to women in succeeding issues. Like her father, her grandfather, and her Gonzales cousins, she had arrived by natural stages of interest and ability at a position of editorial management. Although the position was shortlived, it placed her for a few months in that special group of women editors, including Margaret Fuller, who had helped edit the *Dial*, and the indomitable Sarah Hale of *Godey's Ladies' Book*. Had the publication found a readier audience and firmer financial backing, Elliott's role might have borne greater fruit: the *Quarterly's* obviously liberal cast placed the very worthwhile little publication far ahead of its time for the South. With the demise of the *Forensic Quarterly Review* after its fourth issue, however, she once again turned to a more active participation in the Suffrage Association of her state.

Unlike the more celebrated Fugitive Group of neoagrarians who sprang up in 1930 at rival Vanderbilt University, the Sewanee group in the *Forensic Quarterly* cast its lot with the party of the future rather than the party of the past. It offered one of the most liberal exchanges of views anywhere in the South in its time, joining Henry W. Grady's editorial crusade for economic recovery. Although both the Vanderbilt and the Sewanee groups were seeking a responsible regionalism, the Fugitives sought the answer through deemphasizing material progress; they were antiscience and antitechnology. The Sewanee group in 1909 recognized that the ends of social justice must be served by economic means before the fruits of the spirit could be cultivated. Both groups were examining the doctrine of progress in the light of Christian humanism. If the *Forensic Quarterly* had received a better reception and a wider audience, perhaps industrialization in the South might have taken a less exploitative direction and the Fugitives would not have had occasion to recoil from it so drastically.

It is entirely fitting that Elliott should have had a hand in the *Forensic's* publication, and fitting, too, that it should have been accorded such an obscure fate. The contents of the *Forensic* reflected much of what she had lived and thought and written in

fiction for the past thirty years—liberal, optimistic, ever hopeful for
man to live up to his best ideals—and doomed to be largely ignored.
Gradually, however, many of the causes for which Elliott had
struggled began to reach fruition. She knew, when the South helped
carry the election for Wilson in 1912, that she was far from being
alone as a Southern liberal.

IV "We *People*"

With the end of Radical Reconstruction in the South in 1876, the
old-line aristocrats returned to power, "redeemed" the state legislature from outsiders, and returned to "home rule." Their restoration
to power earned them the label *Bourbons,* after the French royal
line which returned from exile in 1814. While paying lip-service to
the old Lost Cause, many of the so-called Bourbons—men such as
Henry W. Grady of the *Atlanta Constitution,* who led the crusade
for economic recovery through industrialization—also looked to the
future. Whatever else this restoration to power of the descendants
of the planter aristocracy might mean, everyone knew where he
stood in the rigid Southern caste system, and by what rules politics
would be conducted. The Bourbons insisted upon honesty and
probity in office in exchange for their patronage; a man was either
one of *us* or one of *them.* Many of the values of the old aristocracy
persisted in the South through the 1880s and after. The old Code
Duello had not entirely vanished, for the last famous duel in South
Carolina took place in 1881. Elliott had written several stories on
the subject of dueling, discussed as part of her delineation of the
regional experience (Chapter 3), but most of these stories dealt with
an earlier age when the practice seemed somehow less barbaric.
Surprisingly, as late as 1910 Elliott was able to get a story on the
subject of dueling, "Readjustments," about the relationship between an elderly member of the Bourbon class and his son, a youth
who refuses to pay allegiance to the old codes, printed in *Harper's
Monthly.*

This only son of an ancient and now impoverished Southern
family has been reared by an elderly father determined to make his
son practice the manly pursuits of hunting, shooting, and riding as
befits the scion of an aristocratic house. The boy has been afraid of
his father ever since his father punished him for proving "gun shy"
on his first hunt. Since then, the old man has abandoned him to the
care of servants, ridiculed him, and called him "molly coddle."

The solitary youth, an avid reader among the books in the family library, has weighed the old values and rejected them. Against his father's wishes, he has chosen to make writing his life's work and has recently received a check for sale of a story to a national magazine. The old man receives this news with scorn, saying that such work is unsuitable for any son of his. Soon after, a false accusation leads the father to challenge his accuser to a duel. The boy knows his father is too old for such a confrontation and therefore, in a misguided attempt to prove his manliness and save his father, he takes up the hated gun he never wished to fire and goes out to meet his father's enemy. When the old man arrives in town, he finds his only son has been mortally wounded defending the family name. Too late, the father realizes his failure to recognize the boy's genuine talents, so different from his own. He lives on, paralyzed by a stroke, to ponder a lifetime of mistakes. The cavalier code is shown at last to be irrevocably bankrupt, though its vestiges paralyze an entire class and rob it of its intellectual and creative vigor.

Among her unpublished manuscripts, Elliott left yet another story of the Code Duello and its persistence in the South. This story, entitled "*We* People," might well rank with her best, even though the circumstances under which it was written precluded publication.

The title "*We* People" is a phrase used by the Gullah-speaking servant Judy in the story to refer to the Bourbon aristocrats, who, if patronizing, were nonetheless predictable and lived by well-understood rules and customs which gave stability in an age of changing allegiances.

The story opens with a description of the "Sand Bar," a sandbank in the middle of a river, where duelists once met to settle their differences. This notorious sand bar has claimed the lives of Mrs. Weatherly's husband and oldest son, and now there is a chance that it will claim a third victim, for the Code Duello is still practiced here.

Ironically setting the tone of this bloody tale, the author remarks that for the moment in this part of the deep South the Negro Question is quiescent, "broken only by an occasional lynching" (2). Politics are in ferment, however, over the rise to power of a man named Doby, a Populist of obscure origins. Richard Boulton, a Bourbon, has just discovered that Doby has misappropriated funds from a philanthropic trust, and he intends to expose Doby in the public press. Dan Weatherly, Boulton's friend, warns that Doby will promptly challenge Boulton to a duel when the crime is made public, but Boulton declares he does not believe in dueling and will not fight. He wishes the infamous "Sand Bar" could be obliterated from the earth "to do away with this barbarous blood-code" (4).

Doby's efforts to bribe Boulton fail and the exposé is carried out; Doby's response is a written challenge, but Boulton returns it unopened. Doby is livid and issues threats in public. Only Dan Weatherly knows Boulton's feelings on dueling, but will not reveal them for fear Boulton will be branded a coward. He says publicly that Boulton will not fight Doby because Doby is of a class beneath him and no gentleman. Doby ought to be shot on sight, the hot-headed Weatherly declares, for having stolen public funds.

"I've no reason to shoot Doby, and if he shoots me, he'll give me no chance to defend myself" (8), admits Boulton, who refuses to carry firearms, trusting the power of public opinion to put Doby behind bars. One day, however, as Boulton and Weatherly cross a street, Doby steps forth from a doorway, takes aim and fires at Boulton, delivering two more shots as Boulton falls. The wounded Boulton lingers for several days but dies before the arraignment and trial of Doby can begin.

At the trial a "bought" jury of Doby's friends acquit him on the grounds that he shot in self-defense in spite of testimony that Boulton was unarmed. Boulton's friends are outraged, and Weatherly declares that such a miscarriage of justice must be settled by the "code." Old Judy, the housekeeper, finds a note revealing what Weatherly plans but hides it, hoping Boulton's brother Ned, as next of kin, will do the honorable thing and avenge Boulton's death. When Ned fails to act, declaring against dueling in any form, Weatherly gathers a "jury" of twelve friends and rides out at midnight. Next day Doby is found shot twelve times, each bullet from a different gun. The story concludes with Old Judy muttering darkly that Ned Boulton is a coward for failing to carry out his obligation to settle the affair according to the code of "*we* people."

While the medieval values represented in the story chill the reader, even more chilling is the realization that Elliott had once again based a story on historic fact drawn directly from her own experience. The latest form of the Code Duello was "shooting on sight." The shooting incident in the story is based on the assassination of Elliott's cousin N. G. Gonzales in 1903.

The Gonzales brothers, already introduced in Elliott's biography, were a constant source of reassurance to Sarah Elliott regarding her own progressive views, because she saw so many of them expressed editorially in the Gonzaleses' crusading newspaper the *State*. This paper had grown under the editorship of N. G. Gonzales and his brother William from a small-town daily into an aggressive regional voice so powerful that it helped swing Southern votes to Woodrow Wilson in 1912. During his period of editorship, N. G. Gonzales became the principal spokesman in South Carolina for social and political reform of every kind, for public and higher education, for development of mineral resources and diversified agriculture, and for economic progress through railroad and river commerce.

A member of the aristocratic Bourbon class, he was not a tool of the Conservatives, as might be expected, but stood for honest, efficient government and an enlightened progressivism. In *Stormy Petrel* (1973) Lewis Pinckney Jones has documented the career of this grandson of William Elliott III and his bitter fight against the high-handed and dishonest politics of "Pitchfork Ben" Tillman of Edgefield, South Carolina. Tillman was a self-styled friend of the farmer and agrarian leader, who took over the state Democratic party and became governor in 1890.[14]

Gonzales attacked Tillman's Populist claims, saying that "farmers . . . were poorer than they were fifteen years ago . . . ," but Tillman successfully rallied a coalition of farmers and politicians in South Carolina's version of the national agragrian revolt of the 1880s and 1890s (115). Public opinion was divided for and against Tillman along class lines, ranging the Bourbons against the Tillmanites, supporters of this "one-eyed rustic" (118).

Finally, in 1903, the governor's nephew, Lieutenant-Governor James H. Tillman, took matters into his own hands. One day following an especially virulent editorial by Gonzales against the governor, Jim Tillman stepped from a doorway near the state capitol and fired upon the unarmed Gonzales, who died three days later. In a celebrated legal battle, so fraught with political overtones that the trial had to be venued outside the city of Columbia, Tillman was acquitted on the strength of testimony by his "witnesses" that he had fired in self-defense. The jury reasoned that Tillman deserved acquittal because, under the Code Duello, a man was entitled, in South Carolina, at least, to defend his name, even though dueling per se was unlawful.[15]

The death of N. G. Gonzales made the Code Duello more than a matter of principle; as in other Carolina families, it meant personal tragedy. It was, moreover, a great loss for the cause of liberalism.

In Sada's story, as in real life, the ironic twist is that the murdered man's friends know his strong feelings against dueling and that he always deliberately went about without a weapon. Names are changed in the story, of course, but the content is faithful to the newspaper accounts of N. G. Gonzales's death. The notoriety of the case throughout the nation made the short story impossible to place.

Although Elliott exploited the dramatic possibilities of these incidents of dueling, her own view of them is expressed in the words of her character Boulton, who deplores all such acts of violence. By exposing them to public scrutiny she hoped to see them expunged forever from Southern life, like the "Sand Bar," scene of that "barbarous blood-code." Such vestiges of the old code of honor—intemperate language, acts of violence, and mob vengeance—could only perpetuate the old political and social abuses and slow progress so desperately needed by the New South.

CHAPTER 5

Woman's Rights

F EMINIST writings during the first half of the nineteenth century concentrated more on "woman's wrongs" than on "woman's
rights" and were often tangled in with other issues such as antislav-
ery and temperance literature. Never popular in the South, the
cause of equality of the sexes did not emerge as a strong theme in
stories and novels by Southerners until after 1900, except for the
veiled complaints of unhappy heroines in the domestic novels of
such writers as Mrs. E. D. E. N. Southworth.

Sarah Barnwell Elliott's first novel, *The Felmeres*, which shares
many features with those sentimental domestic novels, cloaks
feminist arguments in a story dealing largely with conflicting religious beliefs. The wrongs suffered by Helen Felmere, however,
parallel the complaints articulated by the new movement organized
at Seneca Falls, New York, in 1848 to further the cause of woman's
rights: the demand for educational opportunities, freedom to choose
an occupation and receive equal pay for it, to have full legal and
social status in every sphere of life.

In her last novel, *The Making of Jane*, Elliott creates the New
Woman as the main character, endows her with intelligence,
enterprise, a career, financial independence, and the opportunity to
accept marriage only if it is to be a partnership in which she has full
control of her own future. This type of character appears with minor
variations in two other short novels and several short stories which
will be discussed here. Increasingly, however, as Elliott became
more deeply involved with various suffrage efforts after 1900, she
gave up the medium of fiction and argued woman's rights issues in
essays, speeches, and a widely circulated "manifesto" which helped
to promote ratification of the Nineteenth Amendment in her home
state of Tennessee.

Elliott was thus one of the first and most vigorous proponents of
woman's rights among Southern writers, an advocacy which more

131

than likely hurt her popularity among Southern readers, as J. B. Henneman noted in 1903 when discussing *The Making of Jane*. The Southern attitude toward women came in direct conflict with Elliott's views as well as her own life-style and was one of the reasons for her move to New York City in 1895. She held to her convictions all the same, for she had long ago come to terms with the fact that the time for a return to liberalism in the South had not yet arrived.

I   *Feminist Theories*

"When a woman gives up all idea of matrimony, she either turns saint or woman's rights," wrote Sada Elliott at twenty-two, knowing that in "sneering down" matrimony she was flying in the face of one of the most cherished traditions of the Old South—the Cult of Southern Womanhood.

Attitudes toward women in the South, says Clement Eaton, were derived at least in part from the romantic novels of Sir Walter Scott. The exaggerated courtesy and courtly behavior toward women were not altogether social games, however; these conventions reinforced the strength of family life by limiting the role of woman to wife and mother. While women were idolized, protected, even fought over, they had almost no part in decisions regarding their own lives.[1] And, according to George W. Bagby, a Virginia writer, a woman was "to feed, to clothe, to teach, to guide, to comfort, to nurse, to provide for and to watch over a great household and keep its complex machinery in noiseless order—these were the rights which she asserted, and there was no one to dispute; this was her mission, and none ever dared to question it."[2]

The world of the Southern woman of good family was thus narrowly circumscribed, its boundaries set by social convention, legal barriers, and lack of educational opportunity. Yet recent studies have shown that even within this narrow world many women proved themselves far from helpless. In their isolated homes, planters' wives were often called upon to act as administrators, overseeing large properties. This was especially true of widows, and those whose husbands were frequently absent.[3] The wife of William Elliott III, for example, directed his affairs over long periods whenever he traveled "for his health."[4] Habersham Elliott tells how the estate of his maternal grandfather was managed by his widowed grandmother with the help of Anthony, a respected black slave overseer, who kept all the plantation accounts and records for her until the young sons came of age.[5]

Lack of education, which reinforced the fiction of their physical weakness and intellectual shallowness, was the most serious problem for women under this system. Little girls were usually given sedentary occupations like sewing rather than activities which demanded physical strength and coordination. Instead of mathematics, the sciences, and rhetoric, they were taught singing and given piano lessons, along with a smattering of history and sometimes foreign languages. They were encouraged to dress and dance well and to carry on light conversation but not to discuss serious subjects like religion and politics. They were not to express any strongly held opinions, inasmuch as these were considered "unladylike."

Although there were a few schools for young women in the South as early as 1819, most were female seminaries or "finishing schools" rather than colleges. The school at Montpelier founded by Bishop Elliott was a church-sponsored female seminary of this kind, but it was exceptional in having a fine faculty and an unusually rigorous academic program for women. All such schools shared the problem of fund raising, for no one would endow or support them adequately. In the early 1880s many all-female colleges began to spring up throughout the South, but women were not admitted to four-year colleges and universities until the end of the nineteenth century. When women like Sada Elliott did attend lectures at major universities such as Johns Hopkins, their names were generally not entered on the college rosters.

The lives of unmarried gentlewomen were even more restricted than those of their married sisters. Since woman's role was defined by marriage, the unmarried woman had no status. If she had an independent income, which was rare, a woman might live alone on her own property, as did Sada Elliott's Aunt Esther. Even so, a single woman almost never traveled alone. Such a woman was therefore bound close to home unless she could find work as a teacher or governess. More often, she lacked financial means, and, reliant on the charity of other family members, was relegated like Miss Eliza in Elliott's story to the role of children's nurse or companion to the elderly and ailing.[6] Often unskilled in actual domestic chores, she filled her life with sewing and other handwork, and her social outlets were confined to church circles and family gatherings.

Even if a Southern woman were to have chosen an independent life, there would have been few occupations open to her. In the 1830s Harriet Martineau found only seven occupations open to women: teaching, keeping boarders, needlework, working in textile mills and book binderies, typesetting, and domestic service.[7] The last four of these were not considered proper for a Southern woman. Southern girls, according to Clement Eaton, were taught "modesty, respect for parents, and abhorrence of the conduct of the 'strong-minded' women of the North who advocated women's rights."[8]

Older women as well as men seem to have reinforced this narrow code. The young female maverick who tried to unharness herself from such a burdensome tradition was exposed to constant and unremitting criticism by all the members of the household. In Mary Johnston's *Hagar* (1913), Hagar Ashendyne—a young woman reared on a Virginia plantation by conservative grandparents—is subjected to continual verbal abuse by her grandmother, aunts, and teachers for her advanced notions about woman's rights and her unconventional life-style as a writer. Like Sada Elliott and many of her female characters, Hagar expresses strong opinions, holds tenaciously to the goal of work and financial independence, and rejects marriage for a professional career. Though widely acclaimed in New York and abroad for her literary successes, Hagar is reviled at home for these same achievements. When she becomes a speaker and writer for woman suffrage, Hagar separates herself irrevocably from the values of her family, and from her cousin-suitor, Ralph Coltsworth.[9]

In the Southern mind, the woman's rights issue was associated from the beginning not only with the "strong-minded women of the North" but also with the abolition of slavery. One of the earliest to articulate this link between the position of women and the position of the black slave in America was that observant English traveler Harriet Martineau.[10] The same idea was also stated very early by the Grimké sisters of Charleston, South Carolina, both in their feminist writings and their writings on abolition. In 1836 Angelina Grimké published "An Appeal to the Christian Women of the South," emphasizing the powerlessness of Southern women to influence public policy but urging them nonetheless to read, study, and discuss the issues of slavery, which were so clearly inimical to Christian belief. She encouraged women not to obey Southern laws regarding slaves.[11] So violent was the reaction in Charleston to Angelina's paper that it was burned along with other abolitionist material, and Angelina's family was warned of the danger if she attempted to return home.[12] Two years later, when Sarah Grimké wrote a series of letters on the status of women, she deliberately tried not to associate woman's rights issues with abolition, but the two issues were already closely associated in Southern minds. Wherever they were read outside the South, Sarah Grimké's *Letters on the Equality of the Sexes and the Condition of Women* (1838) soon became important documents in the woman's rights movement.[13] Within the South they were proscribed and then forgotten.

Of the other writers on the position of women in the nineteenth century, including Mary Wollstonecraft in England[14] and Margaret Fuller in America,[15] perhaps the most effective of all was the British philosopher John Stuart Mill, who published *On the Subjection of Women* in 1869. Mill's wife and longtime companion, Harriet Taylor, had advanced most of the original arguments, leaving it to Mill to write them down. It was Harriet Taylor who added to the other feminist arguments the case for giving women the vote. Mill's book was read on both sides of the Atlantic for its well-reasoned arguments and its clear and persuasive style and wit. In some minds it undoubtedly carried greater weight because it was written by a man.

II *Feminism in Fiction*

There is no direct evidence to show which feminist writings Sada Elliott had read by 1870, when she stood upon the threshold of making her own life choices. It is probable that she had read most of the writers mentioned above, even the Grimké *Letters on the Equality of the Sexes*. Many of the chief arguments of the feminist canon are touched upon in Elliott's first novel, *The Felmeres*, suggesting that she had done wide reading and had given considerable thought to these subjects. When *The Felmeres* appeared, it was read primarily as a religious novel. Though an occasional critic commented upon the heroine's strength of character, no one pointed out the ways in which Helen Felmere's situation typified the feminist arguments. Neither was it remarked that her fate resulted as much from the status of women at mid-century as from the status of religious orthodoxy.

Several aspects of Helen's character mark her as a New Woman: her unusual education, her independent attitude, her refusal to live as a social butterfly but to give herself meaningful work to do, her utter honesty, and her refusal to compromise her principles. Of her education, for example, Helen's husband, Philip, comments early in the novel that his wife was "educated far beyond most of the women he knew, and [was] withall gentle and ladylike."[16]

Helen's role in life is determined for her. Her marriage to her cousin is more or less arranged by her father and her scheming future mother-in-law as a way of keeping the Felmere property in the family. At one point she pleads for independence: "Let me stay as I am, I do not wish to marry."[17] But her plea is denied. She tells her future husband she does not love him, but goes through with the legal steps for marriage so long as she is permitted to remain with her father until his death, thus achieving a few more years of independence.

Though finding love with her artist-friend Felix Gordon is out of the question, Helen gains from him hope for the future where women are concerned. "To me it is an age of progress," Felix says of the nineteenth century, "of liberal thought and fearless investigation; an age wherein old creeds will die, and the world will be liberated from all the old trammels of ignorance and superstition . . . ."[18] Presumably a woman might even hope to defy convention by rejecting marriage, as have Felix's sisters, "the ladies singleheart," one of whom is an artist, one a musician. Both lead happy, busy lives.

After marriage Helen finds herself constantly at odds with her female relatives. Whereas they are interested in social affairs and material possessions, indulging in backbiting and insincere remarks, Helen is quiet, retiring, honest, and interested only in her child and in her painting. She defends single women who join religious orders to serve others. She chooses as best friend a woman who shuns social pretensions just as she does.

Helen's painting is shown to be no mere pastime but a serious occupation when she wins a prize for the strong allegorical quality of her work. About other matters, such as religion, she holds strong convictions and defends them with almost masculine vigor. She is so committed, in fact, that once she has decided what is best for her child, she is willing to give him up rather than harm his future because of her own beliefs.

The question of property, and a woman's right to own it separately from her husband, is frequently mentioned in the novel. Because Helen owns her property outright, she can seek legal separation from her husband and go home to live—a choice seldom available to Victorian women. The property will be left to her son at her death, but it is not shared by her husband.

The topics of *The Felmeres* are the issues of feminism. The inferiority and helplessness of women, their supposed lack of learning and strong convictions, their enforced acquiescence to the will of their husbands, their questionable property rights, their inability to determine their children's future all constitute the status of Victorian women against which the feminist rebelled. Helen Felmere is neither unique nor even very original as a feminist character. Hawthorne had endowed two of his more famous heroines with qualities similar to hers. Both Hester Prynne in *The Scarlet Letter* (1850) and Zenobia of *The Blithedale Romance* (1852) are similarly strong-willed, intelligent tradition breakers who assert their rights as human beings in the face of a more conservative, rigorous moral standard.

Hannah Warren, heroine of Elliott's *The Durket Sperret*, though not so tragic a figure as Helen Felmere, also shares some of these same independent traits. She is strong enough to hold out against what must inevitably be an unhappy marriage with high-tempered, narrow-minded, liquor-loving Si Durket. Because she must support her grandparents, she engages in peddling, the only honest work she can find. She knows she could have made a success of her peddling venture if she had been permitted to continue it. She reads and improves herself and quickly acquires knowledge of the world during summer work in one of the university faculty homes. She is proud and self-sufficient, and she considers hard work and a single life far better than a bad marriage.

Not all the Elliott women characters are intelligent, decisive, self-reliant, and businesslike. The spectrum of female characters in her fiction runs from the scheming and spiteful cousin Jane Saunders in *The Making of Jane* to the long-suffering and forgiving Ann Miller in the late short story "Miss Ann's Victory." There are brave mothers and helpless aunts, hard-working mountaineer women, and wealthy young heiresses. The traditional roles of wives and mothers are all explored with emphasis on the patience, courage, and endurance of women. In "Beside Still Waters," a widowed mother waits anxiously for word of a son believed lost in a boating accident. In "The Wreck" a son long thought to be killed or lost in the war returns to find his mother eager to welcome and forgive her "prodigal son."[19] In "Last Flash" an elderly widow, who has seen husband and sons go off to three wars, is persuaded out of her mourning to begin knitting socks once again for the young men called to fight in World War I.[20]

These traditional women characters are ennobled by hardship and suffering. They resign themselves to whatever sorrows and difficulties life brings and, like the old mother in the story "Progress," are sustained by inner strengths that come from their early training and religious convictions. Their courage and endurance hold the fabric of their society together.

Only a few female characters in Elliott's stories and novels are vain, spiteful, overtly unkind or evil, like Grandma Warren of *The Durket Sperret* or Jane Saunders of *The Making of Jane*. In "Miss Ann's Victory" a character named Jane Osborne deliberately maligns her friend in order to steal her beau. Though retribution may take many years, in Elliott's account books these characters usually get their "comeuppance" when old scores are finally settled.

Elliott was most uncomfortable when trying to portray a saintly character like the gentle Beatrice of *John Paget*. Beatrice is so innocent, so good, so ephemeral as to be unreal and unconvincing—more an embodiment of orthodox religious beliefs than a flesh-and-blood woman. Beyond a doubt, the characters Elliott preferred were independent, self-reliant, intelligent ones— Helen Felmere, Hannah Warren, Hetty Lachlan, and Jane Ormonde. Students of the changing role of women will find such Elliott characters most interesting to study.

III *The Domestic Novel*

Though Elliott professed to despise the American sentimental domestic novel, she had undoubtedly read many of them herself. These novels had their own version of the feminist story to tell. Occasionally there can even be found in them a character like the New Woman. Especially popular with Southern readers was Mrs. E. D. E. N. Southworth. Mrs. Southworth entered the already-expanding field of domestic fiction with her novel *Retribution* in 1849. She followed it with nine more highly sentimental works, in which wife-desertion often plays a prominent part. In these scenes of morbid domesticity, which are fairly representative of the genre, the wife is always depicted as victim of her husband's whims or rages, suffering hardships that are often compared intentionally with those of the black slave. To free the heroine from her tribulation,

Mrs. Southworth resorted to the unwholesome device of giving her a husband who was either sick, maimed, absent, doddering with age, or dead. Sometimes Mrs. Southworth made her heroine a child bride married to a man both aged and undemanding; early in the story the child bride would soon enjoy the liberating status of widowhood.

Such stories were enormously popular among women in the nineteenth century, according to Helen Papashvily, who has studied them in detail.[21] Readers identified with the pitiful, suffering heroines through every trial and marital tribulation. Papashvily argues that the burdened wife's dream-wish of escape from her trials, usually made real by the illness or death of the spouse, was a statement of the basic tenet of the woman's rights movement. Papashvily feels that the growing interest in woman's rights provided the motivation both for writing and for reading the domestic novel of the day.[22]

These novels were at the height of their popularity in the year Sada Elliott was born (1848), but the sentimental plots were no longer in fashion by the time her own work began to be published. Yet every writer of the 1880s and 1890s was well aware of the large female readership to which he or she must successfully appeal; these writers also knew what had been on the literary bill of fare for the last half-century. Elliott's work is not entirely devoid of elements found in these domestic novels. Her most successful novel, *Jerry*, for example, begins with scenes of wife and child abuse which result in the death of Jerry's mother and his flight through the mountains. The plot of *The Felmeres* revolves around a woman's legal right to determine her child's future and ends with the tragic death of the heroine. Helen Felmere at least is spared the lingering, fashionable death of consumption brought on by the domestic novel's formula-plot ingredients of suffering and privation.

Elliott does not routinely kill off her male characters or render them impotent, as many sentimental novelists were murderously prone to do. Always preferring men to women friends herself, she treats male characters rather well as a group. There is an occasional villain like Claude Paget to offset the almost saintly goodness of his twin brother, John. Paul Henley of *Jerry* and the double-dealing suitor Mark Witting of *The Making of Jane* both retain their health and vigor to the end of the story despite their villainy. There are fully as many villainous women as there are men characters. Elliott makes neither sex appear appallingly bad nor unbelievably righ-

teous. Their mixed good and evil is an improvement on the view of
humanity presented in the domestic novel.

In "Fortune's Vassals" (1899) Elliott employs the domestic novel
devices of the absent husband and a companionate marriage. The
husband in this story does not appear until the end. He is discovered to have married a liberated young woman writer because he is
an old friend of the family and has promised her father to protect
her. The lady writer is left free to live where she likes while
completing a novel.

The character of the New Woman can be found in domestic
novels well ahead of Sada's Helen Felmere and Jane Ormonde.
Earlier in the century one encounters such a heroine in Mrs.
Southworth's most popular novel, *Capitola: Or the Hidden Hand*
(1859). Capitola is a waif who has been adopted by elderly relatives.
Although pretty and womanly in appearance, she is made to behave
in a boyish manner and at one point even disguises herself as a boy;
she has the courage to fight a duel, abhors sentiment, and talks back
to her elders. She is healthy and vigorous rather than sickly and
languishing. A dash and assertiveness mark her for a New Woman
well ahead of her time. She seeks to achieve sexual equality through
direct competition with men—by behaving, in fact, like a pretty,
impish boy.

Elliott's last novel, *The Making of Jane*, can be seen to have its
origin also in the rags-to-riches formula of such domestic novels as
Marion Harland's *Sunnybank* and the novels of Augusta Jane Evans.
These "scribbling women," as Hawthorne dubbed them, were
aware of the envy female readers felt for male freedom and mobility.
They were also reflecting a real-life trend toward better education
and employment opportunities for women in the latter part of the
century.

IV A Bachelor Lady

Preferring independence both for herself and for her favorite
women characters, Elliott chose to earn her own living as a writer.
She had no wish to be a burden to her brothers, who had families of
their own, and she scorned the idleness of many women, especially
those wealthy women who occupied themselves with trivial social
activities. More than once in her novels she pictured such women in
a most unfavorable light. Instead, she chose the life of a "bachelor
lady," a term she uses in her notebooks in preference to "spin-

ster." She forcefully rejected being cast for life as the supernumerary aunt with nothing to do but spin or sew.

A single life and a professional career were eminently wise choices for one who was by nature "not very intimate with anything but her own shadow" and not a little "obstinate . . . and supercilious" and opinionated to boot.[23] Her time was largely her own, so that she could pursue a writing career unfettered by problems of child-rearing. Before the development of adequate means of birth control, there were few professional women who could combine marriage and a career. Most were unmarried or widowed and childless. Single women with inherited money had few problems, but for those without money work was both a necessity and more and more a source of pride.

The Civil War left behind thousands of unmarried women or widows in the South who were compelled to support themselves; they ran farms, operated businesses, and took up other occupations. Among many changes the war had accelerated were opportunities for women to do work other than housekeeping, to find paid employment as an alternative to dependence on relatives. Also, new educational opportunity meant new jobs for women as teachers, and other professions were gradually opening to them as well.[24]

Elliott presented some of the positive values of being free and self-supporting in her novelette "Fortune's Vassals." The opening scene reveals Hetty Lachlan, a would-be writer, arranging the third-floor studio she has just rented following her arrival in the small town of Dilworth. She is vague about her background, and her air of self-sufficiency lends her a certain mystery. Hetty has a trained voice and joins the choir of the local church, where her talent soon creates such a stir that attendance doubles at every service. She becomes the center of the busiest social season ever witnessed in Dilworth.

Both David Laird and the Curate Bayard are constant escorts for this quiet, obviously well-brought-up young woman. Hetty gives neither suitor any encouragement but maintains a friendly distance, trying to preserve her privacy for work on her book. Oddly, she will not sing for money but donates her choir fee to an evening adult-education school which she helps the curate teach one night a week. Gradually, as she enters more and more into the town's activities, her mysterious background is forgotten.

At Easter Hetty's year of apprenticeship as a writer is up, and she leaves for New York to deliver her novel to a publisher. Upon her return she receives two proposals of marriage but gently declines them both. To David Laird she is finally compelled to reveal her background.

Hetty has been reared by an embittered father whose opera-singer wife deserted him. Hetty has never been allowed to have women companions and has grown up "a man's woman," physically active, strong minded, fair, and honest. She is pretty and well groomed but has the energy and mannerisms of a young boy. Encouraged to develop the naturally fine voice she has inherited, she perfects her singing but promises her father never to go on the lyric stage because of his memories of an unhappy marriage to a career woman. Instead, she has decided to try to become a writer and has arranged to live in a town where she is not known and can work in privacy.

Finally, the reader learns that she is actually already married to a friend of her father, a man much older than herself, who regards her more as a ward than a wife, and who has given her his name to prevent gossip. Because of this arrangement, she has freedom to develop her talents and maintain her independent life-style. She must pay for this unconventionality, however, in disrupted friendships and personal loneliness. She is too advanced for her time.

The story never quite rings true because it is based on what amounts to the young woman's deception about her true identity. The story strains too hard to be "modern" in its presentation of an unconventional style of marriage. One interesting feature incorporated into the novelette is the portrait of Elliott herself setting up her own rented rooms to begin life over again as an independent person in a strange city. The opening scene has many correspondences with her diary entries describing her first feelings and experiences upon arriving in New York City in 1895.

The character of the self-sufficient woman is much better shown in Elliott's last novel, *The Making of Jane*, which shares with her other novels the theme of personal freedom and personal growth. *The Making of Jane* is in every sense a woman's-rights novel, although its heroine is the antithesis of a militant suffragette.

Jane Ormonde is the oldest child of an aristocratic but poor Southern family. She has been adopted by her father's cousin Henry Saunders and the latter's wife, Jane, a childless couple living in New York. Henry has a generous desire to help his overburdened relatives by giving their oldest child every advantage of education, travel, and entrée to the best society. Mrs. Saunders, on the other hand, is a cold, self-centered, domineering woman. Her only interest in the child is to arrange a brilliant marriage for her which will flatter Jane Saunders's own vanity and cause her to appear kind and generous in the eyes of her wealthy friends.

Jane Ormonde is completely dominated by this insensitive and often cruel cousin, who insists upon choosing the girl's clothes, her books, her pastimes, her social engagements, and finally even her suitors. The child's utter honesty and her few attempts to assert her own personality are viewed as obstinacy. Says the older woman, "You are making both yourself and me ridiculous . . . you must change your manner, must cease to be so literal. . . . I would prefer a little slang, a little scandal; anything would be better than this goody-goodiness."[25]

Jane endures this treatment as best she can until she finds herself a grown-up young lady with two very eligible suitors. Her easiest path would be to marry the dashing but penniless Mark Witting, whom she loves. But Mark Witting soon proves himself unworthy by courting both Jane Ormonde and, in secret, her older cousin Jane Saunders in order to win some of the Saunders money to pay his debts. Creswick, the less aggressive but more gentlemanly and generous suitor, truly loves Jane and hopes that in time she will bring herself to return his good-humored and unselfish affection. Everyone acknowledges, "He'd be good for her . . . and give her more liberty in one day than she has had in all her life put together" (108).

Mark Witting suddenly departs for Europe rather than reveal how deeply he is indebted to Jane Saunders for loans she has made to him. Mrs. Saunders blames Jane for failing to accept either suitor, missing entirely her chances for a society marriage. Jane realizes for the first time the shallowness of her cousin's motives and resolves to go away rather than accept the Saunders' generosity without being able to do what they expect of her. She resolves to try to work hard and lead a life more in keeping with the honesty and self-sacrifice of her natural parents. She secretly answers an advertisement and is hired as a teacher for a small private school in the mid-South. Leaving behind only a forwarding address, she packs her trunk with her oldest clothes and runs away to begin a new life. She revels in her freedom: "Free—think of it!—free to come and go; free to be poor, to starve if she liked . . . what a marvelous thing she had done!" (263).

Meanwhile, Mrs. Saunders seeks to recoup her losses by bringing forward Jane's younger sister Marion, telling all her friends that Jane has proven to be stubborn and ungrateful. Marion is thrust into the marriage market and is soon engaged to Creswick. Writing home to Jane's parents, Jane Saunders rationalizes: "But of course, in the world she has met the new woman, and I am afraid that this headstrong movement is the result" (287).

Beaton, one of Jane's employers, belittles her efforts to make her way in the world alone with arguments that are still surprisingly current: "The great cry now is that everything is open to women, and the poor things believe it. There are colleges and the like, but what then? After you are educated, after you have passed all the examinations, you are women still—you *will* fall in love" (351). He goes on to point out that, even granting mental equality and educational equality, men would never have faith in a woman physician or lawyer and would not even hire women as clerks except for the fact that they will work for lower wages. Beaton concludes that it is only the plain women who will work, for the attractive ones will always find husbands. "Women are not meant to go into business . . . and women will never be promoted for fear you will marry, and we'd have to begin all over again on another candidate" (353).

Jane's anger and chagrin at learning that Mrs. Saunders has tricked Creswick into proposing to her sister make her resolve to push ahead and try for success in business. First she opens a millinery shop, and then gives up both the shop and the school in order to accept Beaton's offer of a partnership in a new business. She becomes a department head and is soon promoted to general manager. As her year of hard work begins to show results, she concurs with Beaton that women will have to learn to take life in a different way, not to become upset at disappointments but to struggle on, and, "if in this case our sisters and daughters, and wives grow to be as hard as nails, we'll have to grin and bear it—as I said before, change our taste in women" (398).

Pledging herself to personal success, Jane acquires gradually that calm and deliberation she seeks, and a little of the hardness that will help in times of disappointment. Through it all she refuses to ask for help from her anxious parents, but prefers to struggle on alone. After little more than a year she is able to pay back her debts and finds herself earning a handsome profit from her investment.

On summer holiday at a fashionable seaside resort, she is brought back in touch with her former friends, from whom she learns the real reason for Mark Witting's sudden departure. She also learns that Creswick, having suffered financial reverses, is no longer engaged to her sister. Finally, by chance, she meets Creswick himself and discovers her cousin's deception. Creswick still loves her and appreciates her for her accomplishments. She accepts his offer of marriage, knowing she has proven that a woman can be successful in her own right. Her life with Creswick will not be one of dependence but one in which she can utilize much of her newly developed ability. Jane concludes, "I have made mistakes, but I have learned that life must be lived, and to live it to any effect, we must live it calmly. I have learned to rise above hatred; I have learned not to despair" (431).

How much more numerous were the options open for Jane Ormonde's life in 1901 than for Helen Felmere's in 1879. This later optimistic novel with its happy ending reflects the great social changes which were being wrought by the strength and persistence of the woman's rights movement. It appeared just as the suffrage cause was gaining headway throughout the United States and England. Holt issued a second printing of the book in 1912 as the national women's organizations were gaining momentum for passage of the Nineteenth Amendment. The novel is the undoubted progenitor of Mary Johnston's *Hagar* (1913), and Jane Ormonde is also the spiritual forerunner of Ellen Glasgow's memorable Dorinda Oakley in *Barren Ground* (1925).

One important aspect of the novel is the examination of various kinds of marriages. The first of these is represented by Jane's real parents, a loving and devoted couple, burdened financially with too many children and too little cash. Despite hardships, they work together to keep their land and hold their family together. By contrast there is the loveless marriage of the dominating Jane Saunders and her weak, unassertive husband, Henry. Theirs is marriage at its worst. There are even hints of Mrs. Saunders's infidelity. She has used her young ward as a screen for her own affair with Mark Witting. It is borne home to Jane Ormonde that money and social position mean nothing without love and mutual respect in marriage. Jane wants her own marriage, if she chooses to marry at all, to be an alliance between equals who respect, support, and encourage one another. In Mrs. Saunders, Elliott created one of her few villainesses, a study in selfishness and repressed emotions. The potential viciousness in some females of the species is given long and careful scrutiny, together with an analysis of the destructive power of an unhappy marital relationship.

Elliott wanted to show how marriage could become a prison for both men and women under these conditions. No woman should have to enter a loveless marriage for economic reasons. Rather, the opportunity for mutual support and personal growth should be the goal in marriage, with the woman sharing in and contributing to the family finances. Nor did success in business or a profession necessarily preclude marriage for a woman. Jane Ormonde manages to have her business success and also what promises to be a truly honest, happy, and mutually fulfilling marriage.

V *Woman Suffrage*

By the first decade of the twentieth century the worldwide woman's rights cause had formulated four basic demands for human rights, according to an early historian of the movement, Kaethe Shirmacher: 1. "In the field of education and instruction: to enjoy the same educational opportunities as those of men." 2. "In the field of labor: freedom to choose any occupation; and equal pay for the same work." 3. "In the field of civil law: the wife should be given the full status of a legal person before the law, and full civil ability. In criminal law: the repeal of all regulations discriminating against women. The legal responsibility of man in sexual matters. In public law: woman's suffrage." 4. "In the social field: recognition of the high value of woman's domestic and social work, and the incompleteness, harshness, and one-sidedness of every circle of man's activity from which woman is excluded."[26]

Woman suffrage had emerged as the most militant of these issues, one for which women the world over were organizing to fight. At the International Woman's Suffrage Congress in 1904, Carrie Chapman Catt, an outstanding American suffrage leader, had been elected president. Now for the first time American women were beginning to play a prominent part in the international movement and to share the militancy of their suffragette sisters in England.

In 1910 Elliott addressed this subject in an essay entitled "A Study of Woman and Civilization," written for the *Forensic Quarterly*. The essay begins with a discussion of the new militants and their methods:

These Suffragettes seem to be a new kind of woman, and to their sisters comes the anxious dread that women are not making the best of the freedom granted them so late in time; comes the wonder if what women have done for Civilization in these later centuries, has been done only because they were under the shelter of poised control. If in opening the door of woman's convention-closed cage, man is to find himself face to face with a Tigress . . . let us look a little into these new tactics of this most patient of all animals. Let us examine what through the ages woman has done to advance the Human Race."[27]

Elliott then traces the contributions of woman through earliest civilizations, through the age of chivalry to the seemingly more enlightened present. She shows woman as the food gatherer and the preserver of family life, teacher of children, and the ultimate civilizing influence. Since woman is physically the weaker sex, her weapons from ancient times have had to be beauty and temperament. Only a few had beauty. The rest became toys, tyrants, or long-suffering and self-sacrificing drudges. But those traditional weapons have now become largely useless, Sada points out. Society has changed to the point where sons no longer feel obligated to support mothers and sisters, nor do their women want to be a burden on them. Women want to work, but they need training to get proper jobs; they need to attend the best schools, and not be crowded out merely because of their sex. The laws are made to apply equally to all, but women have no say in making or modifying them. She points out that legally women have been placed in the same category with children, criminals, and imbeciles. For every one of the favorite arguments used against giving women the ballot, she gives a cogent and compelling rebuttal. She ends with the thought that women have borne so much for so long that this time they will not give up their fight. Though in one round they may fail, they will try again, if not for themselves then for their children's sakes.

The essay rings with the polished yet emotion-laden rhetoric of the pulpit or the lecture platform. Indeed, it may even have been used in this way, for Elliott was doing considerable public speaking at this time. On January 5, 1911, a few months after the essay was published, she delivered a lecture at a fund-raising event for the Equal Franchise Society in New York, speaking before a large audience on "A Sketch of the History of the Woman Suffrage Movement in the United States."[28] And the time had come when the medium of fiction would no longer serve; her convictions had to be expressed in deeds. The following year she would play a larger part in obtaining legal rights for women than she had ever dreamed at twenty-two when she declared she would reject both matrimony and the public forum.

As more and more women throughout the nation became radicalized by the continued denial of the ballot, two main strategies were developed for achieving the franchise. The first, favored by Woodrow Wilson and many Democrats in Congress, was enfranchisement of women within their own states. The second, more difficult course was supported by many of the national wo- men's organizations: a direct constitutional amendment, the Nineteenth, or Susan B. Anthony, Amendment. In the South attitudes toward the amendment and woman suffrage were divided not only by traditional attitudes toward women but also by the issue of race. While most women wanted the vote to improve their own place in the world, others with very mixed motives sought the vote for *white* women to offset the Negro vote.[29] Suffrage workers organized vigorous campaigns in all the Southern states. Only in Texas, Kentucky, Arkansas, and Tennessee were they eventually successful in gaining ratification of the Nineteenth Amendment.

A. Elizabeth Taylor, who has studied the suffrage effort in indi- vidual states, has described the progress of the suffrage battle in Tennessee, the thirty-sixth and crucial state to ratify. The first important organizational efforts in the South took place in 1906 with the formation of the Southern Woman Suffrage Conference.[30] The purpose of this organization, as with the National American Woman Suffrage Association, was to amend individual state constitutions to allow women to vote for the presidential electors in each state. Elliott served as vice-president of this organization during its forma- tive phase.[31] Suffrage activity had remained dormant in Tennessee until 1906, when the Tennessee Equal Suffrage Association was organized in Memphis. In 1908 the group received assistance from the State Federation of Labor, which endorsed woman suffrage and offered to circulate petitions to state and national legislators.

Gradually women from cities like Chattanooga and Knoxville began to organize equal suffrage groups. The Memphis organization became statewide in character and activities, adding more than seventy societies and memberships by 1919. In 1912 the Nashville League invited the English suffrage leader Sylvia Pankhurst to speak in the South for the first time. In 1913 the Nashville League also invited Sylvia's mother, Emmeline, though many members were unhappy with Mrs. Pankhurst's extreme militancy. Leagues distributed literature and kept up a lively commentary on issues in the larger newspapers of the state, combating with facts and positive arguments the often inflammatory and scurrilous attacks of the antisuffrage groups.

At the annual convention of the Tennessee Equal Suffrage Association on January 10, 1912, Sarah Elliott was elected president. She served vigorously throughout that year and was re-elected at the annual convention January 6, 1913. One of her major accomplishments was laying the groundwork for bringing the National American Woman Suffrage Association annual meeting to Nashville in November 1914, since this meeting brought about an important turning point in the suffrage movement in Tennessee.[32]

In April of 1913, Elliott and Mrs. Guilford Dudley, president of the Nashville league, marched in Washington to interview members of Congress.[33] Soon after, they requested a hearing before the Tennessee Legislature for themselves and their co-workers Laura Clay of Kentucky and Mary Johnston of Virginia. They were received by the legislators and Sarah Barnwell Elliott became the first woman to address the state legislature.[34]

Elliott also prepared and distributed petitions to the governor of Tennessee, the members of Congress, the state legislature, city councils, and other civic leaders stating formally the reasons why women wanted the vote. The petition written by Elliott combines some of the platform statements of the woman's rights movement with wording taken from her 1910 essay "On Woman and Civilization" and ends with a challenge to make Tennessee the first Southern state to grant the franchise to women. The manifesto makes a pointed appeal to the much-vaunted chivalry of Southern men by reminding them that former slaves had had the franchise for more than fifty years while the legislators' mothers, sisters, wives, and daughters were still waiting for their place within the Constitution as full citizens. The manifesto read as follows:

We [women] represent one-half of the entire population.

We are intelligent; we are native born. We are counted by the Constitution [of the United States] as free people, and we are considered as free persons in the basis of representation.

We see that work knows no sex.

We see that pain and sickness know no sex.

We see that starvation and death know no sex.

We see that taxes know no sex.

We see that in the making of laws only, there is sex distinction.

We are punished for the violation of laws without having a voice in the making of laws.

We pay taxes without appeal.

We have awakened to political consciousness by realizing that in trying to do our work for the home we have to follow it out into the world; that in doing so we have come, and helplessly against the laws of the city, the state, the county.

We cannot keep the house clean; we cannot influence the schools; we cannot get equal pay for equal work unless we get the ballot.

Since the organization of this government, we, your mothers, sisters, wives, daughters, have stood in the Constitution with the infant, the alien, the unpardoned criminal, the idiot, the negro. In 1868, the constitutional door was opened to admit the negro to the kingdom of equality. We are still outside.

Now, to you, one of the lawmakers of the land, we bring this petition why we desire and why we should have the ballot.

Let Tennessee have the glory of being the first southern state to acknowledge her women as friends and comrades. Give us the ballot. We deserve it. We are capable of using it for the good of the country.[35]

The speeches, petitions, and newspaper campaigns had their effect. In the next seven years women in Tennessee won the right to vote in municipal and presidential elections. Finally, on August 16, 1920, despite a formidable last-minute campaign by antisuffrage forces, ratification by the Tennessee legislature was officially proclaimed. The Nineteenth Amendment became federal law.

Though divisiveness within the state suffrage organization had caused Elliott to leave it during her second term, her example of leadership and the national perspective she brought to it, together with the ringing phrases of her petition, combined with the subsequent efforts of hundreds of devoted suffrage workers to bring ratification in Tennessee by the narrowest of margins. American women came at last into full citizenship, even though another half century would pass before many of the broader aims of the woman's rights movement would begin to be fully achieved.

CHAPTER 6

The Role of the Realist

IN her critical writing, even more clearly than in her fiction, Elliott pointed out what she believed to be the role of the Realistic writer: nothing less than the mirroring of society to itself, so that there might be appraisal of its faults and a continual "amendment of life." By contrast, she saw the European Realists and determinists bent upon eliminating entirely man's spirit, man's free will, in their fatalistic dissections of society.

It was thus to George Eliot and later to Ibsen that she turned for confirmation of her own views, reinforced by Howells, whose critical stance fostered and sustained American Realism. She chose the role of a "gentle realist," employing whatever technique would involve the reader's mind and emotions and so effect moral and spiritual uplift.

Realism also served, as we have seen, to counter the romantic myths of the antebellum planter's life fostered by writers like Thomas Nelson Page, who capitalized on popular misconceptions about the South. Finally, this same honest endeavor to "set the record straight" extended to a candid appraisal of the effectiveness of her own writing.

I "Rouse and Better the People"

In an essay commissioned by the *Outlook* in 1901, "The Spirit of the Nineteenth Century in Fiction," Elliott analyzed the guiding spirit of past ages as each found expression in narratives, and finally in the novel form. The nineteenth century she called the Age of Science. Fiction, sharing this spirit, came to suffer the *maladie du siècle*, the illness which comes, as she puts it, by eating too much from the tree of knowledge.[1] A writer like George Eliot, she points out, "clearly and consciously works under the modern scientific laws. . . . It was not by mere accident that *Adam Bede* and the

Origin of Species appeared in the same year. George Eliot as well as Darwin is of the great scientific movement of the nineteenth century."[2] Zola and Hardy, she adds, also work with nature's laws but through these laws they seem to have reached fatalism, "because we know everything. The latest ripened fruits of the Tree of Knowledge are Heredity and Environment and these seem to have finished the task of shutting us in . . . and these seem to have bound us hand and foot . . . and our souls have been so analyzed that at last a modern writer talks of the 'value of the flesh,' and of the spirit as 'the flower of the flesh.' How death-dealing—all is flesh!"[3]

In the writings of Zola and Hardy, once the ancestry and the environment of a character have been determined his fate is fixed. But Elliott refused to accept this deterministic view. She refused to accept that spirit had been dissected away. "This vital spark, at least, escapes all laws; and the outlet from this wall of fatalism built up about us . . . must be the doorway of the spirit. Spirit is life; life is force; force is will; and will is free to fight, to conquer, to soar." Believing this, she also believed that fiction ought to lift up mankind and "help us on our way."[4] The European Realists' dissection of life fell short of the whole truth; determinism left too much out: the spirit, the animus that is free will, the will to change. This fact cannot be ignored, she felt, that man is flesh *and* spirit.

Her own "moral dissections" had been intended for the purpose of uplifting mankind, upholding the same missionary purpose manifested by her father and by her brother: what the Anglican Prayer Book calls the "amendment of life," for individuals and for society.

In a revealing essay on the Norwegian playwright Ibsen, published in 1907, Elliott described a kindred spirit whose moral purpose in writing was much like her own—one who had dealt with man's flesh *and* his spirit. She strongly seconded Ibsen's assertion: "A man shares the responsibility and the guilt of the society to which he belongs."[5] Like Ibsen, it was not as an observer of life only that she had tried to write, but as a sharer in the responsibility for the society in which she lived, as one who did not stand apart viewing critically but who enlisted in the fight for freedom on many fronts.

Elliott admired Ibsen's staunch protestantism, his fight for disciplined and responsible freedom:

Being a Realist, he fights with this weapon of Truth first within himself. He knew none better, where to find good and evil, true and false, sweet and bitter; he knew that in each of us all the fundamentals live and move and have their being. . . . He declares: "Everything that I have written has the closest connection with what I have lived through, even if it has not been my own personal experience." Further he declares: "A man's gifts are not a property, they are a duty." Then comes the announcement of his great creed: "A man shares the responsibility and the guilt of the society to which he belongs."[6]

Elliott saw in Ibsen's search for truth and his exploration of free will that he spoke for the individualist who is faithful to his inner vision, who is the judge of his own soul. Like the Anglican, Ibsen saw God as a God of compassion, allowing man free will to win his own salvation. Ibsen's phrase "unto himself enough" implied man's separateness and also constituted a caution that he should not condemn his fellow man. Each man is engaged in his own heroic struggle toward salvation; every man is in a sense a potential hero; every man's life can therefore be triumphant or tragic; tragedy is no longer the fate of kings and princes only. "All or nothing" is the demand of life; there is no compromise; each man exercises the divine right to judge for himself, though he must not try to judge others. This was the message of Ibsen's "Ethan Brand," one that ran counter to the prevailing Calvinism of Norway.

In Ibsen Elliott saw manifested the desire to show truth, do justice, and in this way to "rouse and better the people." His literary efforts were a "moral accomplishment" which bore fruit in a literary nationalism. In pronouncing judgment on Ibsen, she had struck the vein that runs most prominently throughout her own work: the desire to "rouse and better the people," through moral dissections of human character in fiction.

II A Gentle Realist

Though Ibsen was a kindred spirit in artistic purpose, he was not so strong an influence on Sarah Elliott's technique as were the European novelists, especially the British writers of the mid-nineteenth century who wrote novels having a strong moral purpose. Dickens was certainly near the top of her list, for she was an avid reader of his novels and mentions his characters many times in her letters. *Bleak House* was a particular favorite. George Eliot, another favorite, aimed to bring religion and philosophy out of the realm of abstract theory into lives of the mass of mankind through fiction.

In *Adam Bede* George Eliot had announced her intention as a

writer "to give no more than a faithful account of men and things as
they have mirrored themselves in my mind." Her aim was "the
faithful representing of commonplace things," giving a faithful account of her fellow men, to pity and love them as they are, telling
their story simply and without falsity, not forgetting the homely
detail, the ugly and plain, with emphasis upon human feeling.[7] Her
moral and democratic concerns were shared by Elliott, who found in
the older writer her most influential model.

An equally important influence on Elliott's work was William
Dean Howells. In *Criticism and Fiction* (1891), Howells concurred
with George Eliot's concern for the commonplace, for accurate
reportage, and for material with a moral intent. Howells went
beyond this to formulate an aesthetic principle which incorporated
his moral concern. He spoke of rejecting "the artificial and monstrous" in favor of "the unpretentious and the true." He set as criteria
of taste "the simple and the honest: these will always be both
beautiful and good," he said. "What is this idea of the beautiful
which art rests upon and so becomes moral? Beauty exists in the
human spirit and is the beautiful effect which it receives from the
true meaning of things."[8] Howells preferred that the artist choose
his material from what he had known and observed rather than from
that which others had created, and that he then report his experience faithfully. Yet mere reportage, Howells knew, can be only
"mapmaking," and will not truly picture life unless it seeks to
"widen the bounds of sympathy" by indicating the meaning behind
the facts even at the risk of overmoralizing. The writer, he says,
must be like the observant scientist, finding nothing in life in-
significant. Like George Eliot, Howells wished to bring literature
closer to the mass of humanity and to disclose to all men their
likeness to one another. "Let us make them know one another
better," he enjoined, "that they may be all humbled and
strengthened with a sense of their fraternity."[9]

First as editor of the *Atlantic*, then as a columnist for *Harper's*, it
was William Dean Howells who brought together Realism, local
color, and high moral purpose as the major elements of American
fiction. Under his editorial encouragement, the tentative sketch of a
New England or Southern spinster grew into the carefully plotted
short story. That which a family could read together unblushingly in
the parlor was his measure of printability. Consequently, only the
more benign aspects of life come to light. The suffering, vice, and

depravity of the European Realists are softened here under the sepia-toned glow of the parlor gaslight.

Elliott is without doubt a Howells variety of Realist and local colorist. She shared with Eliot and Dickens the moral purpose of the social novelist. Her style is the modified Realism of Howells. It was sober-sided and serious, this Howells Realism, and it seldom utilized the rich folk humor which characterized the earliest local color of Thorpe, Longstreet, Artemus Ward, and others. Though often called witty herself, Elliott seldom applied her humor to her fiction. Her puns, double entendres, and barbed thumbnail portraits of everyone from relatives and neighbors to presidents were reserved for conversation and her enormously entertaining private correspondence. Humor was a tactic for surviving bitter thoughts and hard times; she seemed to regard it as inappropriate to her published work, where irony is used instead for pointing up the incongruities of life.

III   *The Cavalier Myth*

Elliott's material and point of view are drawn largely from her native South, and it is within a regional context that her work must be read. What part, if any, did she play in the developmental process which led to the flowering of the Southern literary renaissance a generation later?

Such writers as Thomas Wolfe, William Faulkner, and Robert Penn Warren did not spring suddenly from the brow of Zeus. They had to build upon, and react to, the regional literature of the local-color writers, native humorists, speech makers, sermon writers, and journalists who preceded them. Louis D. Rubin, Jr., has recently pointed out that while all the important themes and narrative elements which later emerge in Faulkner's *The Bear*, for example, are found in the sporting sketches of William Elliott III, the earlier writer was unable to reveal the universal motifs and symbolic relationships which inhered in the description of these events. Literary convention of the time, together with conditions of Southern life in relation to slavery, would not permit more than a surface treatment of these powerful themes.[10]

In the years following the Civil War, the South's view of itself in literature was bound up in antebellum myth. In his analysis of the Old South and the American character, *Cavalier and Yankee*,

William R. Taylor has shown how social and economic forces contributed toward a popular view of the Southerner, in terms of his origins and domestic institutions, as the mythic Cavalier, the chivalrous "Southron." This literary stereotype of the generous plantation squire dispensing hospitality on his baronial estate, fighting duels, indulging every whim, gradually darkened to become the doomed aristocrat, and finally the cruel, drunken slave owner stubbornly bound on preserving the status quo even to the point of self-destruction. This Janus-faced stock character came into the popular mind partly for reasons historic, partly out of a defensive need for mythmaking by individual writers.[11]

Taylor's portrait of the Cavalier, and his mythic counterpart in the North, the Yankee, is drawn not so much from historical documents as from works of fiction, from novels and the magazine press, where wishful thinking shapes fact. The myth of the Cavalier, Taylor shows, grew partly out of what was viewed as the deficiencies in the character of the Yankee—his materialism and opportunism. Against these were set the qualities of the legendary Southern gentleman: "honor and integrity, indifference to money and business, a decorous concern for the amenities, and a high sense of civic and social responsibility." Taylor is not interested to explore to what degree the composite portrait of the Southern gentleman had basis in fact. His interest is in the projected images and their revelation of national consciousness.

He acknowledges that the legend was created by men like William Wirt who were born outside the planter group and aspired to move within it. Of the rare writings of the planters themselves he has little to say except that they played only a small part in creating the Cavalier legend. Of those within the planter class who wrote about their experience at all, such men as William Elliott III "produced a disciplined elegiac literature in praise of the old style of life, which they saw as a golden age, yet they played a relatively minor part in creating the literary legends which are popularly associated with the Old South. They had little taste for the flamboyant in character or for the historically sentimental. The creation of the impetuous Southern Cavalier and the nostalgic portrayal of plantation life were to be largely the work of men of a different social background."[12]

Yet the myths died hard. Writers like Thomas Nelson Page kept alive in his stories the image of The Great House and its occupants in "Marse Chan" and "Meh Lady," long after William Elliott's day.

Sarah Barnwell Elliott, whose forebears had made the substance of the Southern myth, was always troubled by the exaggerations and false generalizations of that literary legend. An insider who could draw her characters from life, she took pains to paint an accurate picture of prewar life as she knew it, but her fiction is much more concerned with harsher realities of the postwar years. Her portraits of prewar Southern life show a high-minded, bookish, older generation whose children are turning away from plantation life toward the professions. The postwar problems of the destitute landowner are not glamorized, nor are the many painful readjustments that came with giving up old ways minimized.

Many of her short stories are peopled not with aristocrats but with those who made up the largest part of the South: the small farmer, the struggling businessman, the black man or woman, the mountain covite, representing many, if not all, social groups from 1870 to 1900.

Her concern for setting the record straight is elaborated upon in the book review she wrote for the *Sewanee Review* of Francis P. Gaines's *The Southern Plantation, A Study in the Development and Accuracy of a Tradition* (1924). In it she takes Gaines to task for trading on the literary myth while ignoring historical fact. The illusion of the plantation and its owner was created to satisfy an American love of feudalism, according to Gaines, and out of this illusion came the allegory of aristocracy. He excused this "propaganda" because "it served in certain essential respects to reinforce the plantation tradition," though he acknowledges that most of the writers of this exaggerated literature "were not to the plantation manner born." Gaines concluded, "Though it ceased to function less than sixty years ago, it seems so remote that it suggests a different and more resplendent age. The Plantation romance remains our chief social idyl of the past; of an arcadian scheme of existence, less material, less hurried, less prosaically equalitarian, less futile, richer in picturesqueness, festivity, in realized pleasure that recked not of hope or fear or unrejoicing labour."[13]

Elliott angrily retorts, "Then why, in Heaven's name, was it disturbed?"[14] There had been some virtue in that part of the Southern experience represented by plantation life, she insists, quite apart from the evils of the labor system that supported it. If the Southern planter had indeed been the indolent squire of popular myth or the drunken blackguard of Abolition literature, she asks, how then had the South managed to produce in the next generation and export to all parts of America so many persons who had headed corporations, banks, law firms, or who had excelled in other professional or scholarly spheres? The myth of the Cavalier colored over and hid from view the real intellectual qualities and leadership abilities of many Southerners, both men and women, she maintains.

In her view, these myths denied to the planter class in particular any finer instincts or native ability and saw them only in relation to the institution of slavery. Whole chapters of experience and whole spectra of opinions were lumped together under the single heading "planter." Left out were all those who had long questioned either the morality or economic effectiveness of slavery, or those like her father who had ministered in any sincere way to the spiritual needs of blacks. That there had ever been men of more liberal stamp than the Secessionist radicals had been forgotten. Whence, she asks, did Woodrow Wilson and those in the South who elected him suddenly emerge? In the Wilson era, she reminds her readers, the true spirit of the liberal and the intellectual in the South had at long last reemerged. She was hopeful that the nation would one day recognize that which was of real value in the Southern experience, as well as the complexity of those economic and social problems in the midst of which liberalism had struggled to survive.

IV *Literary Journeywork*

Elliott was not at all sanguine about the effectiveness of her own work in reasserting this point of view. In her more self-critical moments she called her writing "manufactured" and mechanical, unable to capture the elusive popular imagination in the same way as had the nostalgic romances of others. Most Southern readers, she knew, were in no mood to be shown any side of life but their former grandeur and their fallen heroes. She felt that her efforts to paint a more realistic picture had not been entirely in vain, however.

At one point she commented in her notebook, "There are certain writers who I believe have been made—built . . . one can see where the joints are, where the windows have been changed— where the staircase has been forgotten and put up in the wrong place. . . . I seem to smell the fresh mortar between the bricks. And because of this belief that writers can be manufactured we have a great deal of well done, but uninteresting mechanical work." After the fragment she had penciled "my own work."[15]

Such a pessimistic view came from one who was always her own severest critic and overlooked much that was valuable in her work. Her convictions were audacious and in advance of her time, and though their presentation fell short of greatness, she made no little contribution to the cause of liberal thinking.

Since she had to be the mainstay and, as she put it, the "short stop" for her family, she had to produce what would sell. She *had* manufactured her stories for this magazine or that. Overall it was competent literary journeywork, and if it lacked the hand of a master builder like Ibsen, still its informing spirit had been a well-intended desire to counter myth with truth and romance with reality in order to illuminate the social history of the too-long silent South.

As we have seen, her perspective had been too close to the scarring events to be fully shaped into art. Of the war itself she wrote hardly a word. Of such then-forbidden subjects as miscegenation, about which she did write, she could not find a publisher. A more balanced view would await the writers of the generation after hers. *Sartoris*, Faulkner's first novel about the South, was published, significantly, in 1929, the year after she died. She and others who had experimented with local color and with Realism had opened a way, but it was left to those who came after to supply the more detached, ironic viewpoint and to supply the broad interpretations and the symbolic significance of all the contradictory elements in a complex and self-divided society.

The Southern local colorists, whose work was so eagerly sought by the national monthly magazines between 1870 and World War I, performed the journeywork of the Southern literary renaissance. Their attempts to record the uniqueness of their region established certain patterns which many of the later writers were to follow: use of the Negro as a central character, the use of dialect to label regional and class differences (best used to fashion a great literary masterpiece in Twain's *Huckleberry Finn*), a preoccupation with violence and death, the themes of struggle for personal freedom and personal identity, and a more imaginative use of natural surroundings in the symbolic framework of ideas.

V *Winnowed by Time: An Appraisal*

Just as laborers in the Southern rice fields once winnowed grain from chaff, so time and changing literary taste have culled what will endure from what is evanescent in the work of Sarah Barnwell Elliott. Lack of demand for feminist subjects and works of moral uplift has caused most of her work to disappear even from library shelves. Lack of serious critical comment at the same time has obscured what was rightfully her due as a precursor of the Southern literary renaissance.

Elliott was never able to achieve the first rank as a regional writer. Her brief national popularity as a novelist rests almost entirely on the hazy populism of *Jerry*. Part of the reason lies in the very practice so widely advocated by the local colorists of "writing from experience." As a Southerner during the time of that region's greatest economic difficulty, she was to a great extent a prisoner of her sex and class. Her human insights, on the other hand, were far richer than those of many of her contemporaries because of her rewarding associations with faculty, students, and visitors at Sewanee, as well as her New York acquaintances and a large and closeknit family. To an uneventful life she added the enrichment of reading and study, so that her imaginative contacts with the world of books and ideas were unusually vast for a nineteenth-century Southern woman. But however she strove to overcome it, and however parsimoniously she hoarded every experience to make the most of it in her writing, her firsthand experience with the world was limited.

A second limiting factor in her work is the very timeliness of some of her plot materials. Railway speculations and suffrage propaganda no longer excite modern readers in quite the same way they did 100 years ago. Yet, though her writing seems mannered today and her plots recount battles long since won, it should be remembered that the changes wrought in American attitudes on such issues as woman's suffrage and legal and economic reforms that benefited workers and extended education to all were brought about in large measure by the men and women who waged these battles for public opinion in the magazines of the day. The magazine writer and the popular novelist played a larger role in directing trends of public taste and opinion than one may realize. "One must never make the mistake of ignoring subliterary fiction, for it is a power in the world," Jay Hubbell has reminded us.[16]

It was an exceptional popular writer, however, who did not somehow become submerged in a single movement, either local color, Naturalism, or feminist propaganda. Sarah Barnwell Elliott tried her hand at all of them, as well as at criticism, biography, drama, and the literary essay, in addition to the Naturalistic novel and the local-color short story. By experimenting with several current literary trends she was able to earn a steady living with her pen and finally gain a measure of recognition and financial independence. Her only legacy had been her intelligence, her religious convictions, a proud name, and a point of view. These she invested well. In so doing, she proved herself a stubborn survivor, able to weather a chaotic period in American national life which left destitute many families and personalities far sturdier than hers: Lanier died discouraged and impoverished; Cable was virtually driven out of the South by his views on the Negro Question. That she succeeded in living by her wits, giving voice to her views through times of such upheaval, is testimony of the strength and resilience of her mind and spirit.

Only one of Elliott's books is in print today.[17] Almost no one can name even one of her titles. Yet hers was a quiet voice speaking with firm but unimpassioned conviction and at times with telling effectiveness. She deserves better at the hands of the literary historian. In a family of published authors, including grandfather, father, and cousins, she alone commanded a national audience, however briefly. Though the niche she made in Southern and national letters is small, it is authentic and deserves to be carved out with her name upon it.

Among Elliott's artistic strengths can be counted her well-chosen (if dated) themes; her ability to create interesting characters by "sketching from life" with sensitivity to the revealing detail; a good narrative sense; and an ear well tuned for capturing and rendering dialogue and dialect speech.

Her artistic limitations include an unfortunate tendency to preach occasionally to her readers and to weaken an otherwise powerful story with an excessively sentimental ending. Her strongest characters tend to be all of one kind, mostly the so-called independent or "new woman." She is unable, when dealing with some of her Southern material, to hold it at arm's length for a more dispassionate treatment. Finally, like most of the regional writers, and like her own literary forebears, she was unable to handle symbolism, except on very rare occasions, and to lift her vision from the plane of everyday life to the universal.

Nevertheless, her work points the direction in which Southern fiction would go for the next thirty years: realistic, preoccupied with the search for identity, and concerned with themes of frustration.

guilt, violence, and death. Her work shows a full awareness of the
South's problems, an overall optimism and a sincere desire to work
toward solutions through education and changes in the political
system. She deals forthrightly with subjects that are difficult for
Southerners to discuss even today: dueling and the exaggerated
code of honor, ancestral pride, lynching, lawlessness, and racial and
social bigotry.

Like Ibsen's work, her best studies deal with individualism, the
Anglican assertion of the need of all persons to work out their own
salvation by faith and through deeds. Each one is alone, must work
out his own salvation alone, try to be merciful, avoid judging others,
all the while seeking to better the common lot through precept and
example. This vision, however partial its realization, believes that,
though life is tragic, there is hope; though there is evil, there is also
much good; and though we see clearly the realities of things as they
are, we do not surrender our ideals. This is the credo of the liberal
thinker, teacher, and writer. This is the tradition in which Sarah
Barnwell Elliott lived and wrote.

Notes and References

Chapter One

1. Only a handful of Southern women became known as writers of fiction before 1900. These included Mrs. E. D. E. N. Southworth, Marian Harland, Grace King, Sherwood Bonner, Augusta Jane Evans Wilson, Mary Noailles Murfree, Kate Chopin, and Ruth McEnery Stuart.

2. Stephen B. Barnwell, *The Story of an American Family* (Marquette, [Mich.], 1969), p. 40.

3. Ibid.

4. Harriet Martineau, *Society in America* (London, 1837), II, 308.

5. James Moultrie, Jr., M.D., *An Eulogium on Stephen Elliott . . .* (Charleston, 1830), pp. 11–40 passim.

6. Stephen Elliott, [Sr.], "Letter to the Members," Charleston Library Society, January 7, 1926 (unpublished letter quoted by Mrs. Taylor Sheetz, Assistant Librarian).

7. Stephen Elliott, Sr., *An Address, Delivered at the Opening of the Medical College of Charleston, S.C., on Monday, November 13, 1826* (Charleston, 1826), p. 11.

8. Louis D. Rubin, Jr., *William Elliott Shoots a Bear* (Baton Rouge, La., 1975), pp. 1–27.

9. Lewis Pinckney Jones, "Carolinians and Cubans: The Elliotts and Gonzales, Their Work and Their Writings," Diss., University of North Carolina 1952, p. 38.

10. William W. Freehling, *Prelude to Civil War: The Nullification Controversy in South Carolina, 1816–1836* (New York, 1965), pp. 268–70, 309–13.

11. Virginius Dabney, *Liberalism in the South* (Chapel Hill, N.C., 1932), passim.

12. "Sarah Barnwell Elliott," *National Cyclopedia of American Biography* (1931), XXI, 65–66. Elliott's birth date is given in a letter to Louisa Arnold, November 13, 1868. She says, "I can hardly realize how old I am . . . twenty on the 29th of this month." Arnold-Appleton Papers, Southern Historical Collection.

13. The Rev. Richard Johnson, "Georgia Episcopal Institute," in George White, ed., *Statistics of the State of Georgia* (Savannah, 1849), p. 80.

14. Thomas M. Hanckel, ed., *Sermons of the Right Reverend Stephen Elliott, D.D., Late Bishop of Georgia, With a Memoir* (New York, 1867), pp. ix–xix.

15. Frederika Bremer, *The Homes of the New World* (New York, 1853), I, 327–30.

16. Ibid., p. 328.

17. Sarah Barnwell Elliott, letter to Anson Phelps Stokes, April 18, 1914; Anson Phelps Stokes Autograph Collection, Yale University Library.

18. R. Habersham Elliott, unpublished MS, Sarah Barnwell Elliott Papers, in the possession of the present writer.

19. "Beside Still Waters," *Youth's Companion*, August 9, 1900, pp. 385–86.

20. H. L. Mencken, "The Sahara of the Bozart," *Prejudices*, Second Series (New York, 1920), pp. 137–38.

21. Stephen Elliott, Sr., letter to Dr. James McBride, May 8, 1815; courtesy of Mrs. Stephen Elliott Puckette, John's Island, S.C.

22. Stephen Elliott, [Jr.], *Address to the Diocesan Convention*, Christ Church (Savannah, 1841), p. 18.

23. Stiles B. Lines, "Slaves and Churchmen," Diss., Columbia University 1960, p. 214.

24. Barnwell, *Story*, p. 66.

25. Stephen Elliott, Sr., *An Address . . .* , p. 11.

26. Charlotte Elliott, letter to R. W. B. Elliott, August 1859; Church Historical Society Microfilm, Austin, Tex.

27. Barnwell, *Story*, p. 200.

28. R. Habersham Elliott, letter to R. W. B. Elliott, January 14, 1861; Church Historical Society Microfilm, Austin, Tex.

29. For a full treatment of this subject see Willie Lee Rose, *Rehearsal for Reconstruction: The Port Royal Experiment* (New York, 1964).

30. R. Habersham Elliott, unpublished MS, p. 31.

31. Eliza Frances Andrews, *The Wartime Journal of a Georgia Girl, 1864–1865* (New York, 1908), pp. 32–33.

32. Edward McCrady, *Domain of the University of the South, 1858–1958*, An Address at Chattanooga, Tenn., March 1958, to the Newcomen Society in North America (Princeton, 1958), pp. 8–20.

33. Richard H. Wilmer, "The Late Bishop of Georgia," in *The Recent Past—from a Southern Point of View* (New York, 1887), pp. 201–42.

34. Sarah Barnwell Elliott, letter to R. Habersham Elliott, October 2, 1866; Elliott Papers, Jessie Ball duPont Library, University of the South, Sewanee, Tenn.

35. John Gibbes Elliott, letter to R. Habersham Elliott, September 4, 1867, Habersham Elliott Papers, Southern Historical Collection, University of North Carolina Library, Chapel Hill, N.C.

36. Diary of Louisa Arnold, 1867–1870, Arnold-Appleton Papers, Southern Historical Collection.

37. Sarah Barnwell Elliott, letter to Louisa Arnold, March 7, 1868; Arnold-Appleton Papers, Southern Historical Collection.

38. Ibid., July 17, 1868.

39. Robert Treat Paine, letter to George Appleton, 1869; Arnold-Appleton Papers, Southern Historical Collection.

40. Andrews, *Wartime Journal*, p. 337 ff.

41. Sarah Barnwell Elliott, letter to Louisa Arnold, July 17, 1868.

42. Ibid., August 16, 1868.

43. Samuel Greene Arnold, letter to Louisa Arnold, December 5, 1869, Arnold-Appleton Papers, Southern Historical Collection.

44. Sarah Barnwell Elliott, letter to R. Habersham Elliott, April 28, 1871; Elliott Papers, Jessie Ball duPont Library.

45. R. Habersham Elliott, letter to Sarah Barnwell Elliott, n.d., Sarah Barnwell Elliott Notebooks.

46. Copies of *The Church Record,* February through May 1884, in which material by Sada Elliott appeared, are preserved on microfilm by the Church Historical Society, Austin, Tex.

47. R. W. B. Elliott, letter to Charlotte Elliott, January 11, 1884, R. W. B. Elliott Papers, Church Historical Society Microfilm.

48. B. Lawton Wiggins, "Sarah Barnwell Elliott," in Alderman et al., eds., *Library of Southern Literature* (Atlanta, 1907), IV, 1553–57.

49. Undated newspaper clipping among Sarah Barnwell Elliott's papers, *circa* 1886.

50. R. Habersham Elliott, letter to Caroline Elliott, December 6, 1886, R. W. B. Elliott Papers, Church Historical Society Microfilm.

51. Sarah Barnwell Elliott, copy of a letter to the *Louisville Courier-Journal,* June 1887; Sarah Barnwell Elliott Notebooks.

52. Lyon N. Richardson, "Constance Fenimore Woolson, 'Novelist Laureate' of America," *South Atlantic Quarterly* 39 (January 1940), 18–36.

53. Henry James, *Partial Portraits* (London, 1919), pp. 179–80.

54. Sarah Barnwell Elliott, copy of a letter to Constance Fenimore Woolson, June 1, 1887; Sarah Barnwell Elliott Notebooks.

55. Sarah Barnwell Elliott, letters to Esther Elliott Shoup, December 1886—August 1887; Francis Asbury Shoup Papers, Southern Historical Collection.

56. Letters about Bishop Elliott were sent to Sarah Elliott at her request. These have been preserved in the R. W. B. Elliott Papers, Church Historical Society.

57. Sarah Barnwell Elliott, letter to Thomas Nelson Page, August 14, 1890; Thomas Nelson Page Collection, Duke University Library, Durham, N.C.

58. "Sarah Barnwell Elliot," *Who's Who in America* (Chicago, 1910), VIII, 591. Also receipts in personal papers for payment of dues to various societies.

59. Sarah Barnwell Elliott, six letters to Arthur Stedman; Arthur Stedman Collection, Columbia University Libraries, New York, N.Y.

60. Sarah Barnwell Elliott, letter to R. Habersham Elliott, July 17, 1898; Elliott Papers, Jessie Ball duPont Library.

61. Ibid.

62. Mrs. Charles McD. Puckette to the present writer, April 14, 1967.

63. R. W. B. Elliott, cable to Sarah Barnwell Elliott, October 7, 1904; Sarah Barnwell Elliott Notebooks.

64. Sarah Barnwell Elliott, letter to R. Habersham Elliott, February 6, 1901, Elliott Papers, Jessie Ball duPont Library.

65. A ticket stub in Sarah Barnwell Elliott's Notebooks gives the date and title of her address.

66. Much of Elliott's effort in this regard is recounted in A. Elizabeth Taylor, *The Woman Suffrage Movement in Tennessee* (New York, 1957), pp. 59–72.

67. Ida Harper, et al., eds., *History of Woman Suffrage* (New York, 1881–1922), VI, 597.

68. Ibid., p. 609.

69. Sarah Barnwell Elliott, letter to Wallace Rice, January 23, 1913; Wallace Rice Collection, Newberry Library, Chicago, Ill.

70. Telegram in Sarah Barnwell Elliott Notebooks.

71. Sarah Barnwell Elliott, letter to R. Habersham Elliott, April 15, 1925; Elliott Papers, Jessie Ball duPont Library.

72. Ibid., September 7, 1925.

73. Sarah Barnwell Elliott, review of Howard W. Odum's *Southern Pioneers, Sewanee Review* 34 (April 1926), 238–39.

74. Louise Finley, "Sarah Barnwell Elliott," unpublished paper read to the Fortnightly Club of Sewanee, May 1944.

75. An interview by the writer with Stephen Elliott Puckette, Sr., July 1967.

Chapter Two

1. C. Vann Woodward, "The Search for Southern Identity," in *The Burden of Southern History*, rev. ed. (Baton Rouge, La., 1968), p. 28.

2. See F. O. Matthiessen, *American Renaissance* (New York, 1941), and R. W. B. Lewis, *The American Adam* (Chicago, 1955).

3. Woodward, p. 136.

4. Ibid.

5. "Father Tabb's Poems," *Sewanee Review* 3 (August 1895), 431-36.

6. *The Felmeres* (Chicago, 1879), p. 6. Further references are supplied in parentheses in the text.

7. See Chapters 1 and 4 for a discussion of Elliott's state of mind in the 1870s; also: letter to Louisa Arnold, September 21, 1868, Arnold-Appleton Papers, Southern Historical Collection.

8. Mary Wollstonecraft, *A Vindication of the Rights of Women* (London, 1792), Ch. IV, V, passim.

9. Review of *The Felmeres, Boston Globe*, July 6, 1879, n. pag.

10. *Boston Journal*, n.d., 1879, n. pag. These and other reviews are preserved in Sarah Barnwell Elliott's Notebooks.

11. R. W. B. Elliott, letter to Charlotte Elliott, June 22, 1883; R. W. B. Elliott Papers, Church Historical Society.

12. Margaret J. Preston, review of *The Felmeres, Southern Churchman* (*circa* summer 1879), in Sarah Barnwell Elliott Notebooks.

13. Review of *The Felmeres, South Atlantic Monthly* (*circa* 1879), 179-81.

14. R. Habersham Elliott, letter to Sarah Barnwell Elliott, June 22, 1879; Sarah Barnwell Elliott Notebooks.

15. This story was first published serially in the *Louisville Courier-Journal* between January 30 and February 27, 1887.

16. "Mrs. Gollyhaw's Candy-stew," in *An Incident and Other Happenings* (New York, 1899), pp. 163–64.

17. Ibid.

18. "The Land of Ham," *Louisville Courier-Journal*, March 21, 1887, p. 4.

19. "Paris to Pisa," *Louisville Courier-Journal*, January 23, 1887, p. 14.

20. "The Land of Ham," p. 4.

21. "Jerusalem," *Louisville Courier-Journal*, April 29, 1887, p. 2.

22. Ibid.

23. Ibid.

24. "An Idle Man," short story bound with *The Durket Sperret* (New York, 1898), p. 221.

25. "As a Little Child," *Independent* 40 (December 8, 1887), 26-28.

26. "A Florentine Idyl," *Independent* 40 (February 2, 1888), 26-29.

27. "Stephen's Margaret," *Independent* 40 (July 5, 1888), 26-28.

Chapter Three

1. Jay Martin, *Harvests of Change: American Literature 1865-1914* (Englewood Cliffs, N.J., 1967), pp. 1-11.

2. Jay Hubbell, *Southern Life in Fiction* (Athens, Ga., 1960), p. 4.

3. Review of Francis P. Gaines's *The Plantation South* in *Sewanee Review* 33 (July 1925), 353-57.

4. "Miss Maria's Revival," *Harper's* 93 (August 1896), 431-36.

5. "Some Data," in *From Dixie*, ed. K. P. Minor (Richmond, Va., 1893), p. 160.

6. Ibid., p. 165.

7. "Miss Ann's Victory," *Harper's Bazar* 31 (April 9, 1898), 317-18.

8. "Hybrid Roses," *Harper's* 113 (August 1906), 434-49.

9. Review of *An Incident and Other Happenings* by Sarah Barnwell Elliott, *Nation*, (August 3, 1899), p. 96.

10. Jones, "Carolinians and Cubans," pp. 430-32.

11. Hyder E. Rollins, "The Negro in the Southern Short Story," *Sewanee Review* 24 (January 1916), 55.

12. Wade H. Hall, *The Smiling Phoenix: Southern Humor from 1865 to 1914* (Gainesville, Fla., 1965), p. 230.

13. Arlin Turner, *George Washington Cable, A Biography* (Durham, N.C., 1956), pp. 152, 222.

14. Ibid., p. 208.

15. "Without the Courts," *Harper's* 98 (March 1899), 575-79.

16. Review of *An Incident and Other Happenings, Nation* (August 3, 1899), p. 96.

17. "A Race That Lives in Mountain Coves," *Ladies' Home Journal* 15 (September 1898), 11.

18. Comment, *Book News* 17 (July 1898), 657.

19. Review of *The Durket Sperret, New York Evening Post,* May 2, 1898.

20. Review of *The Durket Sperret, Charleston News and Courier,* May 1898.

21. "Old Mrs. Dally's Lesson," *Youth's Companion* 78 (December 29, 1904), 660-61.

22. "Moonshine Whiskey," A play copyrighted May 16, 1912; in Sarah Barnwell Elliott Papers.

23. *John Paget* (New York: Henry Holt & Co., 1891), p. 180. Further references are provided in parentheses in the text.

24. Review of Elizabeth Haight's *Life and Letters of James Monroe Taylor, Sewanee Review* 28 (July 1920), 467-72.

Chapter Four

1. "An Ex-brigadier," *Harper's* 80 (May 1890), 888-98.

2. C. Vann Woodward, *Origins of the New South, 1877-1913* (Baton Rouge, La., 1960), pp. 112-41.

3. "Progress," *McClure's* 14 (November 1899), 47.

4. Donald Davidson et al., *I'll Take My Stand: The South and the Agrarian Tradition* (New York, 1930).

5. "Hands All Round," *Book News* 17 (September 1898), 5.

6. Sarah Barnwell Elliott, letter to Thomas Nelson Page, August 14, 1890; Thomas Nelson Page Collection, Duke University Library, Durham, N.C.

7. John Fox, Jr., is said to have used the runaway mountain boy Jerry as the model for his hero Chad Buford in *The Little Shepherd of Kingdom Come* (1903), a story of the Cumberland Mountains during the Civil War.

8. *Jerry* (New York, 1891), p. 254. Further references provided in parentheses in the text.

9. Marion Lack, "The Agrarian Revolt in American Fiction 1865-1900," Thesis, Columbia University, 1946.

10. Ibid., p. 46.

11. Turner, *George W. Cable*, pp. 263-72.

12. William Norman Guthrie, Editorial, *Forensic Quarterly Review* 1 (October 1909), 48-49.

13. "An Epoch-Making Settlement Between Labor and Capital," *Forensic Quarterly Review* 1 (June 1910), 129-44.

14. Lewis Pinckney Jones, *Stormy Petrel*, (Columbia, S.C., 1973), pp. 186–241.

15. Jones, *Stormy Petrel*, gives a full account of the murder and its aftermath together with an illuminating discussion of the Code Duello. See also W. J. Cash, *Mind of the South* (New York, 1951).

Chapter Five

1. Clement Eaton, *The Growth of Southern Civilization, 1790-1860* (New York, 1961), pp. 320-21.

2. Virginius Dabney, *Liberalism in the South* (Chapel Hill, N.C., 1932), p. 360.

3. Anne F. Scott, *The Southern Lady: From Pedestal to Politics, 1830-1930* (Chicago, 1972), pp. 28-37.

4. Jones, "Carolinians and Cubans," pp. 1-40.

5. R. Habersham Elliott, unpublished MS, in the possession of the present writer, p. 6.

6. Scott, *The Southern Lady*, p. 36.

7. Harriet Martineau, *Society in America* (1837), quoted in Alice S. Rossi, *The Feminist Papers: From Adams to de Beauvoir* (New York, 1973), pp. 139-41.

8. Clement Eaton, *The Waning of the Old South Civilization* (Athens, Ga., 1968), p. 168.

9. Mary Johnston, *Hagar* (New York, 1913), passim.

10. Martineau, *Society in America*, in Rossi, p. 124.

11. Angelina Grimké, *Appeal to the Christian Women of the South* (New York. 1838).

12. Gerda Lerner, *The Grimké Sisters from South Carolina: Rebels against Slavery* (Boston, 1967), p. 147.

13. Sarah M. Grimké, *Letters on the Equality of the Sexes and the Condition of Women* (Boston, 1838).

14. Mary Wollstonecraft, *A Vindication of the Rights of Women* (1792, reprinted New York, 1967).

15. Margaret Fuller, *Woman in the Nineteenth Century* (Boston, 1845).

16. *The Felmeres*, p. 40.

17. Ibid., p. 44.

18. Ibid., p. 78.

19. "The Wreck," *Youth's Companion* 81 (December 19, 1907), 637-39.

20. "The Last Flash," *Scribner's* 57 (June 1915), 692-95.

21. See Helen Papashvily, *All the Happy Endings* (New York, 1956).

22. Ibid., pp. 15-24.

23. Sarah Barnwell Elliott, letter to R. Habersham Elliott, April 28, 1871.

24. Scott, *The Southern Lady*, pp. 106-33.

25. *The Making of Jane* (New York, 1901), p. 87. Further references provided in parentheses in the text.

26. Kaethe Shirmacher, *The Modern Woman's Rights Movement: A Historical Survey* (New York, 1912), pp. xiii-iv.

27. "A Study of Woman and Civilization," *Forensic Quarterly Review* 1 (February 1910), 90-91.

28. A ticket stub in Sarah Barnwell Elliott's Notebooks gives the place, date, and title of her lecture.

29. Scott, *The Southern Lady*, p. 182.

30. Taylor, *Woman Suffrage Movement*, p. 25.

31. "Sarah Barnwell Elliott," *National Cyclopedia of American Biography* (1931), XXI, 66.

32. Taylor, pp. 59–67.

33. Ida Harper, et al., eds., *History of Woman Suffrage* (New York, 1881-1922), VI, 609-10.

34. Ibid., pp. 597-98.

35. "Manifesto," *Nashville Banner*, August 17, 1912, quoted by Taylor, pp. 71-72.

Chapter Six

1. "The Spirit of the Nineteenth Century in Fiction," *Outlook* 67 (January 19, 1901), p. 157.

2. Ibid.

3. Ibid., pp. 157–58.

4. Ibid., p. 158.

5. "Ibsen," *Sewanee Review* 15 (January 1907), 75.

6. Ibid., p. 84.

7. George Eliot, "On Realism," in *Adam Bede* (1859), Chapter XVII.

8. William Dean Howells, *Criticism and Fiction* (New York, 1891), pp. 61–62.

9. Ibid., p. 188.

10. Louis D. Rubin, Jr., *William Elliott Shoots a Bear* (Baton Rouge, La., 1975), pp. 1–27.

11. William R. Taylor, *Cavalier and Yankee* (New York, 1963), pp. 13–71, passim.

12. Ibid., p. 42.

13. Review of *The Southern Plantation, A Study in the Development and Accuracy of a Tradition* by Francis P. Gaines, *Sewanee Review* 33 (July 1925), 353–57.

14. Ibid., p. 357.

15. Fragment in Sarah Barnwell Elliott Notebooks, in the possession of the present writer.

16. Jay B. Hubbell, *Southern Life in Fiction* (Athens, Ga., 1960), p. 3.

17. *An Incident and Other Happenings* (1899), reissued by Books for Libraries Press, Short Story Index Reprint Series, 1969.

Selected Bibliography

PRIMARY SOURCES

1. Manuscript Collections

Arnold-Appleton Papers, Southern Historical Collection, University of North Carolina Library, Chapel Hill, North Carolina.

Louisa C. Arnold Journal 1867–1870, Southern Historical Collection, University of North Carolina, Chapel Hill, North Carolina.

Elliott Correspondence, Wartime letters of the sons of Bishop Stephen Elliott, in the possession of Brigadier General Dabney O. Elliott, United States Army, Retired, Washington, D.C.

R. Habersham Elliott Papers 1866–1877, Southern Historical Collection University of North Carolina, Chapel Hill, North Carolina.

R. Habersham Elliott Manuscript, Sarah Barnwell Elliott Papers in the possession of Dr. Clara C. Mackenzie, Cleveland, Ohio.

R. H. Elliott Papers 1866–1925, Letters from Sarah Barnwell Elliott to her brother Habersham, Jessie Ball duPont Library, University of the South, Sewanee, Tennessee.

R. W. B. Elliott Papers, with family letters, copies of the *Church Record*, and Cuban Diary of Bishop Stephen Elliott, on microfilm, Church Historical Society, Austin, Texas.

Sarah Barnwell Elliott Papers, including two unpublished manuscripts: "Sewanee Life," and "E.Q.B.," a poem about the E.Q.B. Club; photographs, clippings, and miscellaneous correspondence. Jessie Ball duPont Library, University of the South, Sewanee, Tennessee.

Sarah Barnwell Elliott Papers, including diary, notebooks, scrapbook, address book, letters, family photographs, and personal documents in the possession of Dr. Clara C. Mackenzie, Cleveland, Ohio.

Thomas Nelson Page Collection, Manuscript Department, Duke University Library, Durham, North Carolina.

Wallace Rice Collection, Newberry Library, Chicago, Illinois.

Francis Asbury Shoup Papers, Southern Historical Collection, University of North Carolina, Chapel Hill, North Carolina.

Arthur Stedman Collection, University Libraries, Columbia University, New York, New York.

Anson Phelps Stokes Autograph Collection, Yale University Library, New Haven, Connecticut.

2. Published Works

A. Novels and Novelettes

"The Durket Sperret." *Scribner's Magazine* 22 (September-November 1897), 372–86, 492–512, 635–52.

The Durket Sperret. New York: Henry Holt & Co., 1898. Reprinted together with "An Idle Man."

The Felmeres. New York: D. Appleton Co., 1879. Reissued by Henry Holt & Co., 1895.

"Fortune's Vassals." *Lippincott's Magazine* 64 (August 1899), 163–253.

"Jerry." *Scribner's Magazine* 7 (June 1890), 715–34; 8 (July-December 1890), 20–40, 184–99, 284–307, 437–52, 569–91, 774–88; 9 (January-May 1891), 65–74, 242–60, 306–20, 489–500, 576–84.

Jerry. New York: Henry Holt & Co., 1891.

John Paget. New York: Henry Holt & Co., 1893.

The Making of Jane. New York: Henry Holt & Co., 1901. Reprinted 1912.

"A Simple Heart." *Independent* 38 (November 4, 1886), 34–37.

A Simple Heart. New York: John Ireland Co., 1887.

B. Biography

Sam Houston. The Beacon Biographies of Eminent Americans. Edited by M. A. De Wolfe Howe. Boston: Small, Maynard & Co., 1900.

C. Play

His Majesty's Servant. A play written in collaboration with Maud Hosford. Copyrighted 1902 as *Master of the King's Company.* Produced as *His Majesty's Servant* at the Imperial Theater, London, October 6, 1904.

D. Poem

"Alone." *Harper's Bazar* 30 (September 15, 1900), 1238. This is the only published poem which has been located, although there are drafts of many poems in Sarah Barnwell Elliott's notebooks.

E. Book Reviews

The Avalanche by Ernest Poole. *Sewanee Review* 32 (October 1924), 503–505.

"Father Tabb's Poems." *Sewanee Review* 3 (May 1895), 431–36.

La Dame de Sainte Hermine by Grace King. *Sewanee Review* 32 (July 1924), 373–74.

The Life and Letters of James Monroe Taylor by Elizabeth Hazelton Haight. *Sewanee Review* 28 (July 1920), 467–72.

The Little Brown Brother by Stanley P. Hyatt. *Sewanee Review* 16 (October 1908), 507–509.

Old and New: Sundry Papers by Charles H. Grandgent. *Sewanee Review* 29 (January 1921), 122–23.

"Two Collections of Verse." *Sewanee Review* 16 (October 1908), 506–507.

"Some Recent Fiction." *Sewanee Review* 3 (November 1894), 90–104.

Southern Pioneers. Edited by Howard W. Odum. *Sewanee Review* 34 (April 1926), 238–39.

The Southern Plantation by Francis P. Gaines. *Sewanee Review* 33 (July 1925), 353–57.

Visiting the Sin by Emma Rayner. *Sewanee Review* 9 (January 1901), 103.

F. Essays and Articles

"An Epoch-Making Settlement Between Labor and Capital." *Forensic Quarterly Review* 1 (June 1910), 129–44. Reprinted by University Press, University of the South, Sewanee, Tennessee, 1910.

"Ibsen." *Sewanee Review* 15 (January 1907), 75–99.

"Manifesto." Woman Suffrage Manifesto 1912. Reprinted in *The Woman Suffrage Movement in Tennessee* by A. Elizabeth Taylor. New York: Bookman Assoc., 1957.

"A Race That Lives in Mountain Coves." *Ladies' Home Journal* 15 (September 1898), 11–12.

"The Sewanee Spirit." *Bulletin of the University of the South*, Sewanee, Tennessee, 13:2 (August 1918).

"Spirit of the Nineteenth Century in Fiction." *Outlook* 67 (January 19, 1901), 153–58.

"A Study of Woman and Civilization." *Forensic Quarterly Review* 1 (February 1910), 90–101.

Travel Letters. *Louisville Courier-Journal* (January 9–August 28, 1887).

    "Loitering in Paris" (January 9, 1887), p. 16.

    "From Paris to Pisa" (January 23, 1887), p. 14.

    "Rome" (February 13, 1887), p. 1.

    "Across the Way" (March 20, 1887), p. 14.

    "The Land of Ham" (March 21, 1887), p. 4.

    "Sights in Egypt" (April 20, 1887), p. 2.

    "Jerusalem" (April 29, 1887), p. 2.

    "Jerusalem the Holy" (May 8, 1887), p. 19.

    "The City of Flowers" (May 12, 1887), p. 3.

    "Florence" (June 5, 1887), p. 16.

    "Etruscan Gods" (June 18, 1887), p. 4.

    "Siena, Italy" (July 3, 1887), p. 14.

    "In the Tyrol" (July 19, 1887), p. 4.

    "Merry England" (August 14, 1887), p. 14.

    "Oxford, England" (August 16, 1887), p. 2.

    "Old England" (August 28, 1887), p. 16.

Unsigned Articles. "Augustine Birrel," Volume IV; "E. B. Browning," Volume V; "Sir Richard Burton," Volume V. *Library of the World's Best Literature.* 30 Vols. Edited by Charles Dudley Warner. New York: R. S. Peale and J. A. Hill Co., 1896–1897.

Unsigned Articles. *Church Record*, San Antonio, Texas, January-May 1884.

G. Short Stories

a. Collections

An Incident and Other Happenings. New York: Harper & Bros. 1899. The following short stories are included in this collection:

"An Incident."

"Miss Maria's Revival."

"Faith and Faithfulness."

"Baldy."

"An Ex-brigadier."

"Squire Kayley's Conclusions."

"Without the Courts."

"Mrs. Gollyhaw's Candy-Stew."

An Incident and Other Happenings. Facsimile edition. Freeport, N.Y.: Books for Libraries Press. Short Story Index Reprint Series, 1969.

b. Individual Stories

"After Long Years." *Youth's Companion* 77 (April 23, 1903), 197-98.

"As a Little Child." *Independent* 39 (December 8, 1887), 26-28.

"Baldy." *Harper's Magazine* 98 (February 1899), 416-22.

"Beside Still Waters." *Youth's Companion* 72 (August 9, 1900), 385-86.

"An Ex-brigadier." *Harper's Magazine* 80 (May 1890), 888-98.

"Faith and Faithfulness." *Harper's Magazine* 93 (October 1896), 791-97.

"A Florentine Idyl." *Independent* 40 (February 2, 1888), 26-29.

"Hands All Round." *Book News* 17 (September 1898), 1-6.

"Hybrid Roses." *Harper's Magazine* 113 (August 1906), 434-49.

"An Idle Man." *Independent* 39 (June 9, 1887), 26-28.

"An Incident." *Harper's Magazine* 96 (February 1898), 458-72.

"Jack Watson—A Character Study." *Current* 6 (September 11, 1886), 164-67.

"Jim's Victory." *Book News* 16 (October 1897), 47-53.

"The Last Flash." *Scribner's Magazine* 57 (June 1915), 692-95.

"A Little Child Shall Lead Them." *Youth's Companion* 76 (December 18, 1902), 649-50.

"Miss Ann's Victory." *Harper's Bazar* 31 (April 9, 1898), 317-18.

"Miss Eliza." *Independent* 39 (March 24, 1887), 26-27.

"Miss Maria's Revival." *Harper's Magazine* 93 (August 1896), 461-67.

"Mrs. Gollyhaw's Candy-stew." *Louisville Courier-Journal* (January-February 1887). A short story published serially in five parts: (January 30, 1887), p. 13; (February 6, 1887), p. 13; (February 13, 1887), p. 16; (February 20, 1887), p. 13; (February 27, 1887), p. 16.

"Old Mrs. Dally's Lesson." *Youth's Companion* 78 (December 29, 1904), 660-61.

"The Opening of the Southwestern Door." *Youth's Companion* 81 (February 28, 1907), 100-101.

"Progress." *McClure's Magazine* 14 (November 1899), 40–47.

"Readjustments." *Harper's Magazine* 120 (May 1910), 824–32.

"Rest Remaineth." *Pilgrim* 1 (circa 1900), n.p. Files of this periodical, published from 1900 to 1907, are incomplete.

"Some Data." *From Dixie.* Edited by Mrs. K. P. Minor. Richmond: West, Johnson & Co., 1893.

"Some Remnants." *Youth's Companion* 75 (April 18, 1901), 198–99.

"Squire Kayley's Conclusions." *Scribner's Magazine* 22 (December 1897), 758-69.

"Stephen's Margaret." *Independent* 40 (July 5, 1888), 26-28.

"Study of Song in Florence." *Harper's Bazar* 36 (March 1902), 215-22.

"What Polly Knew." *Smart Set* 9 (February 1903), 121-23.

"Without the Courts." *Harper's Magazine* 98 (March 1899), 575-79.

"The Wreck." *Youth's Companion* 81 (December 19, 1907), 637-39.

3. Unpublished Manuscripts

The materials listed below are on loan from the late Stephen Elliott Puckette, Sr., to Dr. Clara C. Mackenzie. They will eventually be placed in the collection of Sarah Barnwell Elliott Papers at the University of the South, Sewanee, Tennessee.

A. Novels

"Madeline." Three manuscript versions of an unpublished novel.

"The Santrys." Manuscript of an unpublished novel of more than 495 pages, also titled "The Oldworths."

B. Plays

His Majesty's Servant. Acting copies of a play copyrighted in 1902 under the name *Master of the King's Company*, by Sarah Barnwell Elliott and Maud Hosford.

The Widow Neville. Manuscript of a play by "E. B. Sull."

Moonshine Whiskey. Acting copy of a one-act play, copyrighted May 16, 1912.

C. Short Stories

"The Heart of It."

"The Infinite Wrong." Correspondence dated May 28, 1927, indicates this story by "E. B. Sharas" was accepted for publication by the *Manchester Guardian*, but there is no record of publication, and no extant manuscript.

"A Long Dream."

"Old Ties."

"On the Other Side of the Moon."

"A Quiet Summer."

"A Speculation in Futures."
"*We* People."

SECONDARY SOURCES

ALDERMAN, EDWIN A., et al., eds. *Library of Southern Literature.* 17 vols. Atlanta: Martin and Hoyt Co., 1907, 1923. Indispensable for biographical sketches but indiscriminately inclusive of little-known writers.

BARNWELL, STEPHEN B. *The Story of an American Family.* Marquette, [Mich.]: By the Author, 1969. A major source of information on the Elliotts.

COWIE, ALEXANDER. *The Rise of the American Novel.* New York, Cincinnati: American Book Company, 1948. Discussions of less well known writers of the nineteenth century, including local-color and regional writers and writers of the domestic novel.

FINLEY, LOUISE. "Sarah Barnwell Elliott." Unpublished paper delivered before the Fortnightly Club of Sewanee, May 1944. Jessie Ball duPont Library, University of the South, Sewanee, Tennessee.

HENNEMAN, JOHN BELL. "The National Element in Southern Literature." *Sewanee Review* II (July 1903), 345-66. Cites Sarah Barnwell Elliott among Southern writers for her stories on the Tennessee mountain life, and briefly discusses her last novel, *The Making of Jane.*

JONES, LEWIS PINCKNEY. "Carolinians and Cubans: The Elliotts and Gonzales, Their Work and Their Writings." Diss., University of North Carolina, 1952.

————. *Stormy Petrel: N. G. Gonzales and His State.* Columbia: University of South Carolina Press, 1973. Liberal crusades, fiery personality, and controversial career of South Carolina's foremost journalist. Gonzales was cousin and friend of Sarah Barnwell Elliott and shared many of her liberal tendencies.

LACK, MARION. "The Agrarian Revolt in American Fiction 1865-1900." Master of Arts Thesis, Columbia University, 1946.

LINES, THE REVEREND STILES BAILEY. "Slaves and Churchmen: The Work of the Episcopal Church Among Southern Negroes 1830-1900." Diss., Columbia University, 1960.

PAPASHVILY, HELEN WAITE. *All the Happy Endings: A Study of the Domestic Novel in America, the Women Who Wrote It, the Women Who Read It in the Nineteenth Century.* New York: Harper & Bros., 1956. Points up woman's rights elements in the domestic novel.

ROLLINS, HYDER E. "The Negro in the Southern Short Story." *Sewanee Review* 24 (January 1916), 42-60. Believes the Elliott short story "An Incident" is the first instance where the Negro appears as a criminal in fiction written by a Southerner. Describes other Negro types written about by Elliott and her use of the Gullah dialect of the Carolina low country.

RUBIN, LOUIS D., JR. *William Elliott Shoots a Bear: Essays on the Southern Literary Imagination.* Baton Rouge: Louisiana State University Press, 1975. Shows how Southern attitudes influenced the imaginative litera-ture produced by men like William Elliott III and others.

SCOTT, ANNE FIROR. *The Southern Lady: From Pedestal to Politics 1830-1930.* Chicago: University of Chicago Press, 1970. Study of attitudes toward women in the South and the female struggle for self-determination.

TAYLOR, A. ELIZABETH. *The Woman Suffrage Movement in Tennessee.* New York: Bookman Assoc., 1957. Details Sarah Barnwell Elliott's part in gaining ratification of the Nineteenth Amendment.

WAUCHOPE, GEORGE A. *The Writers of South Carolina.* Columbia, S.C.: The State Company, 1910. Brief critical biographies of Sarah Barnwell Elliott (p. 61) and other South Carolina writers, with excerpts from their works.

WOODWARD, C. VANN. *The Burden of Southern History.* Baton Rouge: Louisiana State University Press, 1960. Defines what he considers unique in Southern experience as part of the development of a national character.

———. *Origins of the New South, 1877-1913.* Vol. IX. *A History of the South.* Edited by Wendell Holmes Stephenson and E. Merton Coul-ter. Baton Rouge: Louisiana State University Press, 1951. Discusses the economic and political developments of the New South, providing background for a reading of Elliott's novel *Jerry.*

WRIGHT, NATHALIA. "Sarah Barnwell Elliott." *Notable American Women 1607-1950.* Vol. I. Edited by Edward T. James, et. al. Cambridge: Belknap Press of Harvard University Press, 1971, pp. 578-79. A recent updating of biographical data and summary of Elliott's career with emphasis on her suffrage activities.

Index

Absalom, Absalom! (Faulkner), 114
Adam Bede (Eliot), 61, 151, 153
Allen, James Lane, 88, 121, 122
Alta Californian, 76
Anthony, Susan B., 148
Appleton, George L., 33
Arnold, Louisa Caroline, 30–33, 66
Arnold, Louisa Caroline G., 30
Arnold, Matthew, 65
Arnold, Samuel G., 30, 33–34
Atlanta Constitution, 126
Atlantic, 84, 154

Bagby, George W., 132
Barnwell, John, 16
Barnwell, Mrs. John, 23
Barren Ground (Glasgow), 145
Bear, The (Faulkner), 155
Bellamy, Edward, 121
Bleak House (Dickens), 153
Blithedale Romance, The (Hawthorne), 137
Bloody Chasm, The (De Forest), 90
Bok, Edward, 98
Bonner, Sherwood, 42, 62
Book News, 26, 48, 91, 100, 113
Botany of South Carolina and Georgia (Stephen Elliott), 17
Bremer, Frederika, 22
Bright, James W., 39
Bull, William, 16, 17
Burden of Southern History, The (Woodward), 58

Cable, George Washington, 42, 60, 62, 71, 83–85, 120, 123, 161
Capitola (Southworth), 140
Carolina Sports (Wm. Elliott III), 18, 84, 89–90
Castleman, Mrs. Alice B., 40

Catt, Carrie C., 146
Cavarlier and Yankee (Taylor), 155
Chattanooga Times, 50
Chauncey, Elihu, 160
Chauncey, Mrs. Elihu, 47
Clay, Laura, 52, 149
"Cobwebs in the Church" (Cable), 123
"Coeur Simple, Un" (Flaubert), 73
Cooke, John Esten, 19
Coolidge, Calvin, 54
Criticism and Fiction (Howells), 154
Current, 38, 72
Cuyler, Mrs. John, 39

Dabney, Virginius, 20
Darwin, Charles, 152
Davis, Jefferson, 28
De Forest, John, 42, 85, 90
Dial, 125
Dickens, Charles, 35, 70, 153, 155
Dudley, Mrs. Guilford, 149

Eaton, Clement, 132, 134
Eggleston, Edward, 122
Eliot, George, 61, 63, 116, 151, 153–55
Elliott, Caroline, 40
Elliott, Charlotte Bull Barnwell (mother), 21–22, 26, 30, 34
Elliott, Charlotte ("Dawtie," sister), 27, 32, 37, 50
Elliott, Esther (sister), 27, 32, 36–37, 42, 54
Elliott, Habersham (brother), 22, 24, 27, 35–37, 48–50, 54–55, 71, 87, 100, 105, 132
Elliott, Hannah, 54
Elliott, Huger, 54
Elliott, John (brother), 26, 34, 37
Elliott, John M., 33
Elliott, Lucy, 34

Elliott, Ralph Emms, 27, 29
Elliott, Robert (brother), 26–27, 33, 36–40, 42, 66, 69, 73, 106
Elliott, R. W. B., 49
Elliott, Sarah Barnwell, life and times, 15–56
  WORKS:
  "Study of Woman and Civilization, A," 21, 124, 146–47, 149
  "Beside Still Waters," 23, 87, 137
  "Faith and Faithfulness," 25, 88
  "Jim's Victory," 26, 91
  Felmeres, The, 31, 36, 41, 44, 60, 63–71, 75, 102, 104, 115, 131, 135–37, 139–40, 145
  Making of Jane, The, 31, 49, 50, 52, 76, 131–32, 137–40, 142–46
  "Rest Remaineth," 31, 33
  "Madeline," 34
  "Jack Watson—A Character Study," 38, 72
  "Simple Heart, A," 39, 72–74, 115
  "Mrs. Gollyhaw's Candy-stew," 39, 74–75
  "As a Little Child," 40, 76, 79–80
  "Florentine Idyl, A," 41, 76, 80
  John Paget, 43–44, 58, 75, 86, 102–106, 108, 138, 139
  Jerry, 43–44, 50, 58, 97, 102, 109, 115–22, 139, 160
  "Fortune's Vassals," 45, 49, 140, 141–42
  Sam Houston, 47, 86, 106–108
  "Hands All Round," 48, 113–14
  "Spirit of the Nineteenth Century in Fiction, The," 48, 151–52
  His Majesty's Servant, 48, 49
  "Widow Neville, The," 49
  "Moonshine Whiskey," 49, 102
  "Manifesto," 52
  "Infinite Wrong, The," 56
  "Wreck, The," 60–61, 137
  "Jim's Victory," 61
  Incident and Other Happenings, An, 74, 86, 93, 95–97, 108
  "Miss Eliza," 76, 78
  "Idle Man, An," 76, 78–79
  · "Stephen's Margaret," 76, 80–81
  "Study of Song in Florence, A," 76, 81
  "Hybrid Roses," 76, 81–82, 90

  Durket Sperret, The, 78, 86, 98–102, 137–38
  "Illusions on the Delectable Hill," 84
  "Miss Maria's Revival," 87
  "Baldy," 87–88
  "Some Data," 88–90, 102
  "Miss Ann's Victory," 90, 137, 138
  "After Long Years," 92
  "Some Remnants," 92
  "Incident, An," 93–95
  "Without the Courts," 93, 96–97
  "Squire Kayley's Conclusions," 93, 95–96
  "Ex-Brigadier, An," 110–11, 112, 115
  "Race That Lives in Mountain Coves, A," 98
  "Little Child Shall Lead Them, A," 101
  "Old Mrs. Dally's Lesson," 101–102
  "Progress," 112, 138
  "Old Ties," 114
  "Speculation in Futures, A," 114
  "Heart of It, The," 114
  "Epoch-Making Settlement Between Labor and Capital, An," 124
  "Readjustments," 126–27
  "We People," 127–30
  "Last Flash," 137–38

Elliott, Stephen (grandfather), 17, 20
Elliott, Stephen (father), 17–18, 20–29, 34, 39, 133
Elliott, Stephen (cousin), 88–89
Elliott, William, 17–18
Elliott, William III, 18–19, 84, 89–90, 129, 155, 156
Emerson, Ralph W., 63
Ethan Brand (Ibsen), 153
Evans, Augusta Jane, 140

Faulkner, William, 18, 59, 111, 114, 122, 155, 159
Fiesco (Wm. Elliott III), 18
Flaubert, Gustave, 61, 73
Forensic Quarterly Review, 51, 123–25, 146
  Freedman's Case in Equity, The" (Cable), 95
From Dixie (Minor, ed.), 88
Fuller, Margaret, 124–25, 135

Gailor, Thomas, 124
Gaines, Francis P., 84, 157
Garland, Hamlin, 122
Georgia Scenes (Longstreet), 19, 84
Gibbes, Robert, 16
Glasgow, Ellen, 122, 145
Godey's Ladies' Book, 125
Gonzales, Ambrose, 19, 125, 128
Gonzales, N. G., 19, 48, 94–95, 109, 125, 128, 130
Gonzales, William, 19, 48, 125, 128
Grady, Henry W., 109, 125–26
Grandissimes (Cable), 42, 71
Grimké, Angelina, 134
Grimké, Sarah, 134–35
Guerry, William Alexander, 124

Habersham, James, 16
Hagar (Johnston), 134, 145
Hale, Sarah, 125
Hall, Wade, 95
Hanckel, Thomas M., 22
Harding, Warren G., 54
Hardy, Thomas, 152
Harland, Marion, 140
Harper's Monthly, 42, 81, 82, 84, 93, 110, 115, 126, 154
Harris, Joel Chandler, 23, 42
Harte, Bret, 72
Harvest of Change (Martin), 83
Hawthorne, Nathaniel, 69, 71, 137, 140
Hazard of New Fortunes, A (Howells), 116
Henneman, J. B., 132
Holt, Henry, 44, 70, 78, 98, 102, 145
Houston, Sam, 47, 86, 106–108
Howe, E. W., 122
Howells, William Dean, 47, 116, 121, 151, 154–55
Hubbell, Jay, 84, 160
Huckleberry Finn (Twain), 159

Ibsen, Henrik, 151–53, 159, 162
I'll Take My Stand (Davidson et al.), 113
Independent, 39–41, 43, 72, 76, 78, 80
"Indians" (Tabb), 88
Innocents Abroad (Twain), 57, 76

Jackson, Andrew, 107
James, Henry, 41, 69

Johnson, Richard, 22
Johnston, Mary, 52, 134, 145, 149
Jones, Lewis Pinckney, 129
Jungle, The (Sinclair), 121

King, Grace, 42

Lack, Marion, 121
Ladies' Home Journal, 98
Lamar, G. B., 21
Lanier, Sidney, 42, 161
Lawton, Alexander, 26
Lea, John M., 106
Legaré, Hugh S., 20
Letters of Agricola, The (Wm. Elliott III), 18
Letters on the Equality of the Sexes (Grimké), 135
Lewis, R. W. B., 59
Life on the Mississippi (Twain), 42
Light in August (Faulkner), 114
Lincoln, Abraham, 27
Lippincott's, 42, 49, 82, 84
Literary News, 69
Longstreet, A. B., 19, 84, 155
Looking Backward (Bellamy), 121
Louisville Courier-Journal, 39, 42, 76
Lover's Tale (Tennyson), 69

Manchester Guardian, 56
Mansfield, Katherine, 80
"Marse Chan" (Page), 83, 156
Martin, Jay, 83
Martineau, Harriet, 17, 134
Matthiessen, F. O., 59
McCabe, W. Gordon, 44
McClure's, 48, 82, 112
McTeague (Norris), 116, 119
"Meh Lady" (Page), 156
Mencken, H. L., 24
Middlemarch (Eliot), 63
Mill, John Stuart, 135
Minor, Mrs. K. P., 88
Modern Language Notes, 39
Murfree, Mary n., 42, 62, 85, 97, 101, 116

Nashville Banner, 52
Nashville Tennessean, 50
Nation, 70, 94, 97

Negro Question, The (Cable), 60, 95
New York Evening Post, 50, 101
New York Times, 50
Norris, Frank, 116, 119

Octopus, The (Norris), 116
Odum, Howard, 54
On the Subjection of Women (Mill), 135
Origin of Species (Darwin), 152
Otey, James H., 28
Outlook, 48, 151

Page, Thomas Nelson, 44, 47, 83, 88, 115, 151, 156
Pankhurst, Emmeline, 149
Pankhurst, Sylvia, 148–49
Papashvily, Helen, 139
Peterson, John, 94
Petigru, James L., 20
Pilgrim, 31
Poe, Edgar Allan, 62
Polk, Leonidas, 28
Preston, Margaret J., 70
Puckette, Charles, 50
Puckette, Charles M., 37, 50
Puckette, Mrs. Charles McD., 48
Puckette, Stephen, 50, 55

Reign of Law (Allen), 122
Retribution (Southworth), 138–39
Rhett, Robert Barnwell, 27
Rice, Wallace, 55
Rodman the Keeper (Woolson), 41, 90
Rollins, Hyder, 94
Rubin, Louis D., Jr., 155

"Sahara of the Bozart, The" (Mencken), 24
Sartoris (Faulkner), 159
Scarlet Letter, The (Hawthorne), 137
Scott, Walter, 19, 132
Scribner's, 42–44, 82, 84, 93, 98, 115
Sewanee Review, 51, 54, 84, 86, 157
Shakespeare, William, 46
Sherman, William T., 27, 91
Shirmacher, Kaethe, 146
Shoup, Francis A., 36, 37, 46
Silas Marner (Eliot), 63
Simms, William Gilmore, 16, 19
Sinclair, Upton, 121

Society in America (Martineau), 17
"Solitude" (Tabb), 88
Southern Churchman, 70
Southern Life in Fiction (Hubbell), 84
Southern Plantation, The (Gaines), 84, 157
Southern Pioneers (Odum), 54
Southern Review, 17, 20
Southworth, E. D. E. N., 138–40
Stanley, H. M., 77
Starkweather, Nettie, 41
State, 19, 94
Stedman, Arthur, 47, 49
Stedman, E. C., 47
Stormy Petrel (Jones), 129
Stribling, T. S., 122
Stuart, Ruth McEnery, 55
Sunnybank (Harland), 140

Tabb, John Bannister, 62, 88
Tales of Uncle Remus (Harris), 23
Taylor, A. Elizabeth, 148
Taylor, Harriet, 135
Taylor, William R., 156
Tennyson, Alfred, 69
Tiger-Lilies (Lanier), 42
Tillman, Ben, 94, 122, 129
Tillman, James H., 129
Timrod, Henry, 20, 42
"To Lucie" (Lanier), 88
Tom Sawyer (Twain), 116
Traveler from Altruria (Howells), 121
Twain, Mark, 42, 57, 71, 76, 121, 159

Van Dyke, Henry W., 47
Victoria, Queen, 34

Waller, Lewis, 48
Ward, Artemus, 155
Warner, Charles Dudley, 46, 47
Warren, Robert Penn, 155
Wiggins, B. Lawton, 86, 108
Wilmer, Richard H., 29
Wilson, Woodrow, 53, 129, 148
Wirt, William, 156
Wolfe, Thomas, 155
Wollstonecraft, Mary, 67, 135
Woodward C. Vann, 58–59, 111
Woolson, Constance F., 41–43, 82, 84–85, 90

Youth's Companion, 87, 92, 101

Zeublin, Charles, 124
Zola, Emile, 61, 152